Knowledge Is Pleasure

RAS CHINA in SHANGHAI

RAS Shanghai series

In 1857 a small group of British and Americans seeking intellectual engagement in a city dedicated to commerce established the Shanghai Literary and Scientific Society. Within a year the organisation was granted affiliation with the Royal Asiatic Society of Great Britain and Ireland in London and the North China Branch of the Royal Asiatic Society was born. The Society was re-convened in Shanghai in 2007.

The RAS China in Shanghai series of China Monographs, published in association with Hong Kong University Press, is designed to reflect the vibrancy as well as the wide research interests and contacts of the Society and to provide a forum for its members and associates to publish their research interests.

Series Editor: Paul French

Other titles in the RAS China in Shanghai series:
Lao She in London by Anne Witchard

Knowledge Is Pleasure

Florence Ayscough in Shanghai

Lindsay Shen

香港大學出版社
HONG KONG UNIVERSITY PRESS

Hong Kong University Press
14/F Hing Wai Centre
7 Tin Wan Praya Road
Aberdeen
Hong Kong
www.hkupress.org

© Hong Kong University Press 2012

ISBN 978-988-8139-59-0

British Library Cataloguing-in-Publication Data
A catalogue record for this book is available from the British Library.

10 9 8 7 6 5 4 3 2 1

Printed and bound by Liang Yu Printing Factory Ltd. in Hong Kong, China

For

Byron (沈慈平)
Ewan (沈天白)
Owen (沈天雨)

Contents

Acknowledgements

Firstly, I am grateful to Paul French, editor of the Royal Asiatic Society in Shanghai, Hong Kong University Press China Monograph series for his enthusiasm and kindness, and commitment to the pleasure of reading. I am grateful too, to Michael Duckworth, publisher at Hong Kong University Press, for undertaking this project, and to May Holdsworth, for her patient attention to the manuscript, and to Jessica Wang for attending to the details of production. I extend a special thanks to the Royal Asiatic Society China in Shanghai, for financial assistance towards the production of this book, as well as for providing a forum for scholarly exchange, support and friendship.

I would like to thank the following people and institutions for their kind assistance and generosity in making available to me documents, correspondence and images:

Elinor Pearlstein, the Art Institute of Chicago; Laurie Dalton, Acadia University Art Gallery, Nova Scotia; David Kessler, The Bancroft Library, University of California, Berkeley; Alessandro Conficoni, The Bridgeman Art Library, London; Dorothea Mordan, Chandler Designs, Woodsboro, MD; The Chicago History Museum; Susan Miller, The Cleveland Museum of Art;

Acknowledgements

Irene Scarratt, Charlotte County Archives, New Brunswick; Lea Osborne, Rare Book and Manuscript Library, Columbia University; Rachel Woody, Freer Gallery of Art and Arthur M. Sackler Gallery Archives, Washington DC; Susan Halpert and Emily Walhout, Houghton Library, Harvard University; Harry Chancey, Kingsbrae Arms Relais & Chateaux, St. Andrews, New Brunswick; Ingrid Larsen; Andrew Loutit; Isa Schaff, Noble and Greenough School, Dedham, Massachusetts; Laurie Ellis, The Schlesinger Library, Harvard University; Joan MacPhail, Laird Books, Regina, Saskatchewan; The Asian Division of the Library of Congress; Sylvie Rollason-Cass, The Newberry Library, Chicago; Eric Politzer; the staff of the Shanghai Library Bibliotheca Zikawei; Paige Mann, University of Redlands, California; Douglas Doe, RISD Archives, Rhode Island; Jessica O'Toole, Special Collections Research Center, Syracuse University Library, New York; Simon Elliot, Manuscripts Division, University of California, Los Angeles; Christine Colburn, University of Chicago Library; Rebecca Schulte, Spencer Research Library, University of Kansas; Kate Hutchens, Special Collections Library, University of Michigan; Robert Mintz, Walters Art Museum, Baltimore; Craig Hadley and Nicollete Meister, Beloit College, Wisconsin.

In addition, I would like to thank the following people for advice, encouragement, and support: Katharine Burnett, Kathleen Campbell, Ian Gow, Peter Hibbard, Judy Hoechner, Li Tiangang, Chloe Li, Liu Wei, Audrey and Ewan Macbeth, Mike Nethercott, Lynn Pan, Peter Sanger, David Sullivan, and Anne Witchard.

Lastly, I owe a debt of thanks to my husband and sons to whom this book is dedicated, and without whom there might never have been a China adventure: Byron, Ewan and Owen Shen.

Introduction
Poise

Winter sunlight glances off the polished fenders of the 'Blue Tiger', parked outside 'the Grass Hut'—a seemingly traditional and prosperously un-hut-like Chinese courtyard house (*Figure 1*). A smartly dressed Western woman with impeccable posture is opening one of the twin planks of gleaming black wood that form the door; carved above her, the classical Chinese poets Li Po and Tu Fu are depicted playing *wei ch'i* or 'hedged-in checkers', while serving boys warm wine over a charcoal brazier. Above this scene of poise and quietude is a band of carved peonies, and surmounting the graceful arcs of the roof, fish flick their tails skywards— symbols of a plentitude that, even judging just from this picture, was so obviously realized in life.

The woman is Florence Wheelock Ayscough. Next month she will be sixty years old. The following year she will marry her second husband, move to Chicago, and, three years later, the site of this house will be occupied—appositely in light of Shanghai's restless evolution—by the New Shanghai Construction Company.

For now, though, it's a perfectly framed moment of stillness. A hiatus. Her demeanor doesn't betray that the previous year she lost her first husband after years of debilitating illness and a

Figure 1 Florence Ayscough outside the Grass Hut, Christmas card, 1934. Special Collections, Armacost Library, University of Redlands.

soul-bruising trek through Europe in search of treatment. This 'traditional' house was built especially for them in 1922–23, and was situated near the northern border of Shanghai's foreign-controlled International Settlement. But there's nothing to suggest the recent tragedy of the Japanese razing of the Chinese-controlled district of Zhabei in the First Shanghai War of 1932, just north-west of this house, or the disquiet among foreigners that their Concession-era lifestyle of privilege may be ending, or the growing tensions that would soon lead to the outbreak of full-scale war between China and Japan. The recipients of this Christmas card would never imagine that surrounding this house are two coal companies, an iron works, a chemical factory and an electrical firm.

Is this Christmas card a subconscious slip? A foreigner's proprietorial hand-on-the-door of traditional China? With the gleaming Blue Tiger as impotent protector of an untenable position? She is, after all, a British woman of substantial wealth and prominent social position.[1] She was born into the Wheelock family—early and pedigreed Western settlers in Shanghai who assembled a comfortable fortune out of freight. Her first husband belonged to all the right clubs and councils, and was part of the foreign-imposed apparatus that governed the city's Western enclave. She is inextricably part of the last gasp of semi-colonialism, much maligned for its conservatism, protection of its own interests, prejudices and inertia in the face of a rising Chinese nationalism.

So firmly entrenched in elite Shanghailander life was her family that its members walk through the pages of the *North China Herald* like familiar characters in a family saga. Here, a prowler slips past their Sikh guard in the night and robs the servants of their umbrellas. There, she sets sail on the *Empress of Asia*, the ship plushly decorated in Louis Quinze, headed for Vancouver. Here, her husband masterfully defuses a heated quarrel at a meeting of the shareholders of the Astor House Hotel Company. There, he bags 34 birds at the Shanghai Gun Club tournament as his wife graciously presents the trophy. Here, he complains in a Letter to the Editor about the ludicrousness of race ponies' names, arguing that the 'plucky little beasts' deserve more respect. There, her sister-in-law sets up a sewing project to help indigent women keep food on their tables; here are her father's golf and her brother Geoffrey's shooting scores.

Against this background of privilege and position, was it then an insensitive jest to call this comfortable house, with its central heating furnace room and plentiful bathrooms a 'grass hut'? There were indeed grass huts close by, but these were the squalid temporary dwellings of recent rural migrants to the city, who squatted on the boundaries of Shanghai's administrative units. By the 1930s these were proliferating in quantity and deteriorating in quality, especially around the railway station not far from the Ayscough residence. On one occasion a grass hut sprouted outside her very door—a temporary shelter for a northern family fleeing a bad harvest.

But Florence Ayscough's Grass Hut belongs in a very different context, as a tribute to the Tang-dynasty poet Tu Fu, who built his own grass hut in eighth-century Chengdu. Ayscough may be a moneyed Westerner who fully partakes of the pleasures of expatriate life, but she is also a remarkable scholar who by Christmas 1934 had just published the second part of a critically acclaimed translation of Tu Fu. During her lifetime she was regarded as one of the most perspicacious and sympathetic sinologists in the English-speaking world. Her 1925 publication *A Chinese Mirror: Being Reflections of the Reality behind Appearance* was widely admired for its ability to render China 'a living entity' to Western readers. Her subsequent translations of classical Chinese poetry—particularly her terse, Modernist translations of Tu Fu—engendered the respect of a great many esteemed literary critics and writers. Later, the American poet Kenneth Rexroth relied on her translations, among others, as the basis for his own work. John Thompson, a major Canadian poet, was deeply influenced by Ayscough's Tu Fu translations.[2] Although Ayscough is hardly a household name now, she made a contribution to modern poetry in English that resonates still.

Ayscough was an energetic woman, whose interests ranged from ethnography to art collecting, photography, gardening and sports. Her writings also attempted to delve into the lives of Chinese women and children—an aspect that has attracted attention from feminist critics. According to her own accounts, the spur to these scholarly activities was her involvement in the North China Branch of the Royal Asiatic Society in Shanghai; she served as its librarian from 1907 to 1922 and was responsible to no small degree for its development as a major literary resource in China. She was a frequent speaker and contributor to the Society's annual *Journal*, and in 1921 was the first woman to be elected as an Honorary Member of the Society.

Because of the autobiographical nature of much of her writing, the preservation of many of her letters, and the Shanghai newspapers' interest in her family, her life story reveals a rare, intimate evocation of a Shanghailander childhood, and of the experiences of a Western woman in Concession-era Shanghai. She lived in China during some of the most momentous episodes in its history, including the overthrow of the Qing dynasty and the establishment of a Republic ('After four thousand years there is no longer a Son of Heaven'). She writes as a historian of culture rather than politics, yet touches on topics still salient, which Chinese people themselves (often with government backing) are reappraising and experiencing anew. Her interests ranged from classical painting to what was then modern Chinese art; she studied famous places and tourist sites and explained how they acquired their layers of meaning; she appreciated intangible culture, and wrote about festivals, customs and popular religion.

Knowledge is Pleasure.[3] Her family and friends often remarked on her joy in the life of the body as well as that of the mind. As a younger woman she rode horses, 'had a splendid physique', sailed, swam in the English Channel and the bracing waters off New Brunswick (though not, as far as we know, in the less restorative currents of the Yangtze). She also revelled in cerebral pursuits, had a 'beautiful and penetrating mind', hunted ideas, flushed out meanings. An early adopter of technology she roamed Shanghai with her hand-held camera, created a collection of meticulously hand-coloured slides, appeared in film and spoke on radio, enthusiastically embraced innovation (she would have flown airplanes if her first husband hadn't so strenuously resisted). Both active and contemplative, she pursued whole-heartedly the enormously ambitious aim of making a seemingly impenetrable culture accessible to Western readers. If wonder is the beginning of philosophy happiness was its end.

Carved above the front door of the Grass Hut, Li Po and Tu Fu enjoy their intellectual puzzle. On a wooden beam in the guest hall is a carving of the Ho Ho twins, who after inventing the abacus, died of laughter.

1
Shanghailanders
Guns, Gardens and Long-gone Houses

In the mid-1930s the American artist Eva Dunlap painted a map of Shanghai, showing the way to her friend Florence Ayscough's home, the Grass Hut, at 72 Penang Road (now Anyuan Road) (*Figure 2*). On her map Dunlap called the house 'Mecca'—a destination for innumerable seekers, and a place she had been welcomed, first as a stranger, then as a close friend. In Shanghai Ayscough had become a discerning host, known not so much for lavish entertainment or the social equity of her guest list (there were plenty of establishments in Shanghai to meet these desires) but instead for the calibre of her conversation, the depth of her knowledge, and her generosity in sharing it. Her guests found her, quite simply, an inspiration. In the room where she entertained she displayed a bowl of pebbles gathered from the Nanjing hills. Her guests seemed to find her as refreshing and enlightening as these 'eye-washing stones' in clear water.

How much of our knowledge is shaped by the places we inhabit? Eva Dunlap's cheerfully idiosyncratic map of Shanghai provides many pointers as to how Ayscough acquired hers. These are the streets and landmarks that formed the backdrop to her life in China, and to the lives of the expatriate readers who were her

Figure 2 Eva Wyman Dunlap, drawing of a map of Shanghai, after a painting by the artist. Reproduced by permission of Dorothea Mordan.

initial audience. But human interactions with place are reciprocal. Shanghai helped form Florence Ayscough, but she and her family also made an impact on the city that was their home over a period of 70 years. Dunlap's map, then, seems a good starting point from which to explore Ayscough's life.

Shanghai's spectacular riverfront, the Bund, is the obvious place of embarkation. A painting dating from 1867–68 depicts the Bund's extraordinary development since 1842, when Shanghai had become one of the five Treaty Ports, opened to British trade and residents who lived in the city under British law and their own administration (extraterritoriality). Twenty five years later, this painting portrays a handsome sweep of buildings fronting the western bank of the Huangpu River, which is bustling with steamships and sailing craft, some under the ensign of the Royal Navy.[1] The breeze moves with soot and the snap of white sails. Between the larger ships scuttle the tenders and tugs that would later remind Ayscough, as a child watching the same scene, of industrious black beetles. The British Consulate presides at the northern tip, a rather modest bulwark for the financial and trading institutions muscling into line to its south. It is clear that commerce instructs governance. The city's major Western shapers are there: Jardine, Matheson and Co., and David Sassoon and Sons, both initially major opium dealers; Russell and Co., the American shipping firm and Dent, Beale and Co., traders in silk and tea (though both earlier opium dealers); the Hongkong and Shanghai Bank and the Oriental Bank, both prestigious British financial institutions; and the bastion of elite British male social life, the Shanghai Club.

Two buildings north of the Shanghai Club on the corner of the Bund and Canton Road (now Guangdong Road) is Wheelock and Company's auction house. In the painting it is a sturdy, blonde-coloured building, but in reality its solidity was a fiction. Already by the 1860s it had become an anachronism, as the Bund evolved from a dockyard lined with warehouses and merchants' living quarters to the site of powerful banks. The warehouses and auction rooms were shuffled behind the Bund; the Wheelock building was soon to move south to the French Bund. Its disappearance from its former position, though, did not signal any reversal of fortune. By the time Florence was born into this family, the company had brought the Wheelocks great fortune and social stature.

Not that they had come from insignificant beginnings to create themselves anew in Shanghai. Florence Ayscough's father, Thomas Reed Wheelock (c.1843–1920), belonged to a prominent Nova Scotia family that could trace its ancestors to the Reverend Ralph Wheelock, a Puritan emigrant to Massachusetts in 1637.[2] A branch of this family moved to Nova Scotia in the mid-eighteenth century. Although most were initially farmers, some established themselves in shipbuilding and maritime trade. By the mid-nineteenth century Florence Ayscough's paternal ancestors were commercially successful and politically and socially well-connected far beyond the boundaries of Nova Scotia; the opening of Shanghai provided the opportunity to expand a business in which they were already proficient. Thomas Reed Wheelock's eldest brother, John Andrews, came to Shanghai in 1853 to work for the merchants Fogg and Company. In April 1861 he set up independently as an auctioneer and agent.[3] Later that year, advertisements were placed in the *North China Herald* for 'Wheelock & Co., Auctioneers, General Commission Agents, and Proprietors of Cargo Boats. Office and Godown in North Gate Street'.[4] Shortly afterwards, another much younger brother, James, came to join his brother (he appears as a city resident in the 1863 Shanghai Almanac). Despite the prospect of untrammeled opportunity, business success in Shanghai was never guaranteed, and was all too easily pre-empted by misadventure or illness. A river accident in the summer of 1862 might have terminated the nascent venture. 'Messrs. Wheelock and Co', as agents for the steamer *Union Star*, recently arrived from California, had invited Shanghai residents on a river cruise. In a dash of hubris, the captain laid on more steam for a burst of speed, blowing out the boiler which caused the decks and saloon to explode. Several of the passengers and crew died; others were seriously injured, and only four were unhurt. 'Mr. Wheelock' escaped with a head injury.[5] It was, though, an incident from which the firm recovered. The youngest brother of the Wheelock family, Thomas Reed, came out to Shanghai to join his elder brothers in 1863.[6]

An off-shoot of the company, created by Thomas Reed, was the Shanghai Tug and Lighter Co. Ltd., which focused on river freight and passenger services. Although Wheelock and Co. certainly had both British and Chinese competitors, by virtue of its size and breadth of operations it came to assume such a position in expatriate society that a fortnightly report of its business was published in the *North China Herald*—the most influential English-language newspaper on the China coast. These reports read as fragmentary snapshots of foreign commerce as it engaged with China's political and climatic instability: 'Owing to the military activity in the Yangtze Valley there has been nothing doing in the coastwise market; reports from the rice districts point to an excellent crop this autumn, provided there is some more rain at an early date.' 'Since last writing we have had another busy fortnight on our Homeward freight market with every prospect of its remaining so, as long as exchange is weak forward.' 'The export trade from the north is in a very bad state: there is little cargo in Tientsin and little or nothing coming from the interior owing to troubles in Mongolia.'

Vicissitudes aside, Thomas Wheelock was to become one of Shanghai's most prominent early Western settlers, and was able to look to New England high society for a bride. Edith Haswell Clarke (1848–1913) was part of a Bostonian family with strong social and intellectual connections. Clarke's uncle, who played an important role in her life after the early death of her father, was a Harvard professor and educational theorist. Although he disapproved of education for women, other female members of the family, ironically, were writers and educators. The Clarke family also had numerous connections with Transcendentalism—a major intellectual tradition in nineteenth-century America. Clarke's father, Manlius Stimson Clarke, had known Henry David Thoreau when both were students in the same graduating class at Harvard.[7] Despite the fact that Florence Ayscough received no formal university education, her background points to an environment of great intellectual curiosity and experimentation.

Thomas Reed Wheelock and Edith Clarke were married in Boston in 1872 and returned to Shanghai where their eldest daughter, Florence was born on 20 January 1875. As the daughter of a Canadian father, who was a British subject, Florence was therefore a China-born Briton. An 1870 census of the International Settlement provides some detail of the society in which the family lived. Britons were the biggest contingent of the 1,666 foreigners, so Florence Wheelock as a British subject was part of a majority, but also quite definitely a minority amongst the Chinese, who had numbered 51,421 in 1870.[8] Five years before her birth there were only 167 foreign children in the city. When Edith Clarke joined her husband in Shanghai she was one of only a few hundred foreign women in a commercially-oriented society in which family life was quite outside the norm. At this time the Wheelocks were atypical amongst foreign residents, and they were certainly a minority among the overall population of the settlement, outnumbered by Chinese by a ratio of 31 to 1.

To return to Eva Dunlap's map, running due west from the Bund is Nanking Road (now Nanjing Road), which beyond the Race Course turns into Bubbling Well Road (now Nanjing West Road), the site of the Wheelock family mansion. In the early 1860s the British residents of Shanghai, yearning for some pastoral relief from their commercial pursuits, created a riding track that stretched towards the famous 'bubbling well', a natural spring long prized by the Chinese residents for its restorative properties. It became a popular recreational byway, and in 1866 was transferred to the British-run Shanghai Municipal Council. Over the next decades it became Shanghai's most salubrious residential neighbourhood. Standing on what is today one of the city's most congested upmarket retail districts, it is difficult to visualize the enormity of these formerly palatial mansions set in their acres of manicured gardens. A 1907 article on the road in the periodical *Social Shanghai* gives some indication of the lavishness and indulgence of these chateaux, tricked out in Tudor, or Romanesque features, adrift in vast lawns and defended by high gates and dense hedges.[9]

By 1907 many of these were already long gone, and short descriptions of her childhood home in a book Ayscough wrote for young readers in the early 1930s, *Firecracker Land*, are all that remain of the Wheelock residence:

> ... when I was small the garden seemed enormous. An oval drive led up to the great creamy-white house, covered with yellow roses. During the short season of their bloom, the gardeners cut them by the hundred. Every morning Mamma arranged them in shallow baskets, and they were piled into the trap

in which Papa drove himself to the office. This was
a high dogcart with red wheels, drawn by a stocky
Mongolian pony. So every morning we watched it
dash round the oval drive, and knew how busy Papa's
office coolies were soon to be delivering the roses to
our friends in Town.[10]

Firecracker Land provides a valuable glimpse into the early childhood of a privileged sojourner.[11] Much of her time seems to have
been spent in this garden, as a wide-eyed girl with long, straight
hair and bangs cut straight across, riding endless solemn miles
on her dainty-footed donkey, Neddie. In the absence of friends
of her own social class, animals such as the 'fearfully clever'
Neddie who collected tributes of sugar at the dining table, the
goose whose beak caressed her ears (and also assaulted men's
trousers), and her Formosan pony Brownie, substituted as her
playmates and confidants. For a city that was later to dazzle for
the succulence of its entertainment, Shanghai's offerings for small
children were remarkably paltry in the 1880s. A highlight was a
travelling circus with one fat white horse, a baby elephant and a
ravishing equestrienne. Florence was smitten. Determined to join
the circus as a bareback rider she created a training arena in the
garden. It is a scene of great bathos. Forbidden by her parents from
leaping off the galloping haunches of Neddie or Brownie, she was
forced to compromise. An inanimate 'pony' was rigged up on the
lawn, from which she leaped through homemade paper hoops.
Disappointment is the mother of resourcefulness.

Apart from a retinue of (mainly male) servants, Ayscough
was very much left to her own devices. She was one of very few
upper-class European children in Shanghai, and later explained
that, regarding familial relations, Chinese and Westerners tended
to mutually reinforce segregation. Western and Chinese children,

not least because of language barriers, were not habitual playmates. Although Ayscough grew up among Chinese household staff, the language in which they communicated was pidgin—the hybrid 'business English' originally developed to aid trade communications. Even later when she spoke Mandarin Chinese fluently, she still spoke pidgin with the Shanghainese, being unable to speak their dialect.

Her father, like the archetypical Shanghailander, was absorbed in business and sport, a man who 'loved his steam launches and his cargo boats almost as much as he did us, his children, and was always dashing about, inspecting, organizing, and visiting ships in his energetic, decided way'. In addition to his ships, he loved his horses and taking his young daughter to visit the two warm rows of yellow-blanketed ponies in his garden's stables. Equine pleasures were a particular indulgence of Shanghai sojourners; in addition to riding, hunting and carriage driving, the keeping of race ponies was a popular though expensive pursuit. One chastened visitor to a charity project run by Ayscough's future sister-in-law realized that his monthly outlay on one pony could sustain a needy family with children each month.[12] It was not a widely made comparison, and, judging from the race coverage in the *North China Herald*, made no impact on equestrian spending. Shanghai was acknowledged as the perfect milieu for such pleasures, as a 1920 guidebook enthused: 'There are few places where the adage "The best thing for the inside of a man is the outside of a horse" is better understood than in Shanghai.'[13] Later, as a young bride in Shanghai Ayscough was very much part of the 'racing set', but love of horses was part of her paternal heritage.

From a child beguiled by horses, she developed into a capable horsewoman, but even as a small child knew the difference between the 'short sharp click' of a China pony's hooves, and the ring of those of a long-limbed horse. She knew how horses moved, and divined how they thought, and this equine knowledge was to sharpen her later translations, such as these lines from Li Po's *Songs of the Marches*, which appeared in her first book *Fir-Flower Tablets* published in 1921:

> Horses!
> Horses!
> Swift as the three dogs' wind!
> Whips stinging the clear air like the sharp calling of
> birds[14]

And in Li Po's lines in *The Sorrel Horse* is the rebounding echo of her experience with her own ponies:

> The sorrel horse with the black tail gallops, gallops,
> and neighs,
> Lifting, curving, his grey-jade hoofs.
> He shies from the flowing water, unwilling to cross,
> As though he feared the mud for his embroidered
> saddle-cloth.[15]

As previously noted, Florence's maternal heritage valued learning, even though her early education was desultory. She learnt French at a local convent, and German from a governess. Her aptitude at languages was already apparent—she reputedly spoke German before she could speak English, and as an adult was able to lecture comfortably on highly literary subjects in both languages. She also learnt the violin from a German musician (her mother played the cello). Again she was gifted; as an adult she played first violin for the Shanghai Philharmonic Society. From her mother she learnt basic literacy and arithmetic—the latter a subject for which she demonstrated far less talent.

She had three younger siblings—Geoffrey Manlius (1879–1920), Marjorie, who was born in 1882 and died as a young child, and Thomas Gordon, known simply as Gordon (1884–1902). None of her siblings play much of a role in her autobiographical writings on childhood, though Geoffrey is mentioned in her adult correspondence and appears in newspapers as one of the Shanghailander set. Her siblings were too young to provide companionship, and like many lonely children she became immersed in the sensory world around her. Her fragments of childhood memories are often intensely visual, sharply focused moments. She is lifted up between two stone dogs to gaze into the 'green bubbling depths' of the famous well a mile from her home; below her beloved aviary was a rose-covered arbour that cast ever-shifting patterns on the ground; she, a solemn child in a red dress sitting on a footstool, looks up at the grey-green colour of her mother's tea-gown. Here is the sensibility that was later to draw her to Imagist poets such as the American Amy Lowell, who was to become her close friend and co-translator, as well as to classical Chinese poetry which is so often composed of highly concentrated, highly charged visual moments.

The natural world provided endless sensory stimulation. The Shanghai of Ayscough's childhood was already the overcrowded city experiencing continual urban transformation and bouts of property speculation, but it was also a city surrounded by countryside, a mesh of creeks, rivers and canals, stretches of open landscape populated only by the dead in the grave mounds that were such an intrinsic feature of rural southern China. There exist maps of the shooting districts around the city, books on country rambles round Shanghai, and contemporary descriptions of the feeding grounds of mallard, widgeon, pintail and teal, only half a mile outside the city walls of nearby Suzhou. The pogroms of the Taiping Rebellion (1850–64) had, for a few decades, turned swathes of the Yangtze Delta into almost deserted stretches of copses, creeks, melancholy deserted villages and grave mounds. These became the playgrounds of Western seekers of sport, leisure, and respite from urban toil.

Recognizing the loneliness of their daughter, Ayscough's parents brought her on the hunting and houseboat trips that were the popular recreational pursuits of privileged Shanghailanders. These houseboats were broad-bellied and flat-bottomed craft, with large sleeping cabins, dressing rooms and small kitchens. A contemporary, J. O. P. Bland, who had come to China to work with the Chinese Imperial Maritime Customs, then the Shanghai Municipal Council, wrote a bombastic though alluring account, *Houseboat Days in China* (1909), in which he lambasted the 'cankerworm of luxury' which led sybaritic Westerners to trick out houseboats like floating villas. The Wheelocks' houseboat *Ariadne* was sufficiently salubrious for it to be lent to Queen Victoria's grandsons, the Duke of Clarence (Prince Albert Victor) and Prince George (the future King George V), an incident that afforded Edith Wheelock momentary mortification. As Ayscough recollects in *Firecracker Land*, on receiving the news her mother gasped, 'My dear Tom, the quilts are not fit to be seen! I can't have the Queen's grandsons use them as they are now!' On this occasion, as on many others, the Wheelocks' dignified and competent Chinese butler interceded, ensuring that the next morning, loaded onto Thomas Wheelock's red-wheeled dogcart, were two softly wadded quilts covered in red and blue shot silk. Incongruously perhaps, this butler, a 'benevolent despot' immaculately dressed in a long silk robe, was found a job as one of Shanghai's principal dairymen when the Wheelocks left China, as a reward for his faithful service.

According to Bland, European houseboats were crewed by 'the pariahs of our floating population', half of whom should have been in hospital and the other half in jail. What Ayscough remembers, though, is the ingenuity of the cook who rustled up marvellous meals from seemingly nothing but chopsticks and a bowl. A cold dinner menu of 'so simple a nature' in a 1906 issue of *Social Shanghai* indicates the expectations of European house-boat guests:

> iced beef tea
> fish-pomfret
> jellied chicken
> herring salad
> cold saddle of lamb
> peach jelly and iced soufflé
> cheese and pulled bread
> iced coffee

Little wonder the young Florence was awed. While her father bagged snipe attempting to migrate to Mongolia, she sat on the forward deck, mesmerized by the landscape. Again, these recollections from childhood are about the essences of things. The autumn countryside,

> ... had the deep purple brown of dead cotton stalks, in the winter it was the softer brown of old grass, and in the spring it was vivid with the yellow of rape and the pink of peach blossom.
>
> At night, curled under one of the famous red silk quilts, I would lie listening to the soft rhythmic thud of feet on the after deck as the crew swung to the *yu-lo* [sculling oar]. The boat made scarcely a ripple as she cut through the dark glassy surface of the canal, but when she was drawn over a fish weir,

> the bamboos brushed under her keel with a most deli-
> cious *swish-sh-sh*.[16]

She sees, she listens, she feels. She observes the world and sometimes in that shift of mind peculiar to childhood (and perhaps her
Transcendentalist forebears) she ceases to be a subject separate
from everything around her. The shrill cries of boatwomen,
hoarse-voiced coolies, boats colliding with a dull thud, the clack of
bamboo poles, the shrieks of small padded children harnessed to
their decks, barking dogs and clucking chickens. All of these things
just are. Maybe her later empathy for Chinese landscape (*shanshui*)
poetry, in which the barriers between the self and non-self dissolve,
had its roots in gently drifting houseboat experiences such as these.

Although her life in Shanghai was circumscribed, she was
an extraordinarily well-travelled child. By the time she was nine
Florence had circled the globe several times, travelling via the
Suez Canal, Italy, France, London, across the Atlantic to Boston,
then from San Francisco to Japan and back to Shanghai. In 1889,
when she was fourteen, her father decided to retire from China,
and so the family returned to Boston, where Ayscough spent the
rest of her adolescence. One of the reasons for this move was to
ensure that the children could attend 'regular' school, as Geoffrey
at least was proving an intractable pupil for his young English
governess. Geoffrey and Gordon in time were to attend Noble and
Greenough School in Boston, established as a preparatory school
for Harvard University.[17] The school Florence attended, though,
was anything but 'regular' and doubtless nurtured the teenager's
supple intellect and independent spirit. Mrs. Quincy Shaw's
School at 6 Marlborough Street had been established by Pauline
Agassiz Shaw, for her own and her neighbours' children. The wife
of mining investor Quincy Adams Shaw, Pauline Shaw was herself

the daughter of the renowned geologist and Harvard professor Louis Agassiz, and step-daughter of Radcliffe College's first president, Elizabeth Cary Agassiz. Pauline Agassiz inherited an enquiring, non-conformist spirit, and was active in the Women's Suffrage movement, prison reform and progressive education (she funded 31 kindergartens and promoted technical education).[18] After running the private co-educational school Ayscough attended, she turned the building into the headquarters of the Massachusetts Woman's Suffrage Association. Ayscough's lifelong interest in women's and children's welfare must have been at least partially encouraged by the pioneering and philanthropic ethos of Pauline Shaw.

During this time in Boston, Ayscough met and was befriended by someone who was to play perhaps the most prominent role in her later personal and professional life. On Commonwealth Avenue near the Wheelock residence at number 283, resided the illustrious Lowells, the 'Boston Brahmins' who had created a fortune and social position from textile manufacturing. Hearing that a small child from China had been seriously ill with pneumonia, Mrs. Lowell sent over cream every day of young Florence's convalescence. Her solid, fresh-faced daughter Amy paid a visit to cheer the wan-faced Florence, and the two became lifelong friends, intimates and eventual collaborators. Although they weren't schoolmates, and they were often separated by oceans and continents, Amy Lowell and Florence Ayscough effectively grew up together. They shared their siblings with each other; Amy Lowell's brothers were Abbott Lawrence Lowell, President of Harvard University from 1909 to 1933, and Percival Lowell, founder of the Lowell Observatory in Flagstaff, Arizona, and also an authority on the Far East.

With Amy Lowell, who was to become notorious for her difficult nature, sexual non-conformity and venomous feuds with poets such as Ezra Pound, Ayscough enjoyed an intimate, platonic friendship. They went together to the Lowell country house, Sevenels, in Brookline (named after the Lowell family's seven members). They took long drives, drove fast horses, engrossed themselves in long conversations against a backdrop of trotting hooves and the whirr of carriage wheels slicing through the Massachusetts autumn leaves.

They experienced young womanhood together, staunchly supportive of each other's amorous adventures and misadventures. When it became apparent that Amy preferred women to men, Florence took it in her stride. A year older than Florence and an emotionally impetuous foil to the latter's measured calm, Amy experienced earlier the headiness of infatuation, the self-abandonment of love affairs, the traumas of broken attachments. Utterly accepting of her friend's lesbian sexuality, Ayscough nursed her through heartbreaks, and tried to patch together troubled relationships. She accompanied the young lovers to various amusements and 'shared those pleasures which convention permitted'. She mentions lectures. In 1912 Lowell met her life partner, the actress Ada Dwyer Russell, with whom she began openly cohabiting in 1914, in an aptly-named 'Boston Marriage'. Lowell's muse, ballast, inspiration to her most charged erotic verse, Russell was to remain one of Ayscough's close friends for the rest of the latter's life.

For her part, Florence enjoyed the more modest attentions of at least one young suitor and briefly considered an attachment, but was cautioned by Lowell, 'never marry any man unless you can't help it'. On that occasion, she didn't.

In addition to their New England life, the Wheelocks also paid prolonged summer visits to St. Andrews, New Brunswick, home of Thomas Wheelock's sister, Isabella Gove. Ayscough had been brought to St. Andrews regularly since early childhood; it contributed resonantly to her childhood education, and became her adult home after Shanghai. A small, picturesque town on a spit of land projecting into the Passamaquoddy Bay, St. Andrews had by the 1890s become a fashionable summer resort for Boston and Montreal high society. Improvements in rail links between New England and the Maritimes led to the building of elegant summer homes and hotels, and the development of facilities for golf, fishing and boating, tennis, cricket and croquet, and sea-bathing. Promoted as a salubrious reprieve from urban modernity, its freedom from quicksand, undertow, sharks and mosquitoes was especially emphasized, as were its benefits for sufferers of hay fever and nervous disorders.[19]

Family ties may have been the primary reason for the Wheelocks' visits, but the physical beauty of the area, its growing status as a playground for the rich, plus its sporting opportunities must have been a significant draw. The local newspaper *The St. Andrews Beacon* provides plenty of information about the family's activities. They golfed, they sailed, they attended fashionable parties. Thomas Wheelock's two young, athletic sons Geoffrey and Gordon battled it out for first prize on the golf links their father had helped create. Florence dazzled at the card table at a party for the town's young and beautiful summer visitors, won a spirited two-hour game of euchre and was awarded one of the 'artistic and well-chosen' prizes that included Wedgwood and Dresden china.

At first the family and their Chinese servants stayed in the town's first summer hotel, The Argyll. The family habitually (if idiosyncratically) travelled abroad with their staff, attracting bemused curiosity over Chinese garb and the incomprehensible patois of this high-status family's pidgin English. Mutual culture shock in Boston: as a 'treat' Ayscough and her mother visit the kitchen where they discover a tramp devouring a hearty breakfast. He counters their astonishment with a reassuring cock of the thumb towards a Chinese manservant, 'the lady in the blue dress' who invited him in.

The rambunctious retinue of family, staff and sporting dogs was too much for The Argyll. In October 1896 *The Beacon* began a rather breathless account of the building of a sumptuous new summer 'cottage' on a site overlooking the town and harbour. *The Beacon* gushed admiringly that as Wheelock had 'made all the money he wants in China' he would now reside in Boston or New York, and summer in St. Andrews.[20] The 'cottage' was a mansion of about nineteen rooms. Its Queen Anne Revival architectural style and wood-shingled cladding were reminiscent of fashionable summer retreats being built at resorts such as Newport, Rhode Island. Despite a break over winter, work progressed so rapidly that by the next June the Wheelocks' cottage 'Topside' was complete, and considered 'one of the prettiest and most commodious in town'. It still exists, sensitively preserved, as the Kingsbrae Arms— an award-winning, intimate hotel surrounded by gardens that still retain the flavour of Ayscough's work there in the 1920s.

Topside's vistas over the bay and its magnificent gardens must have further developed the young Florence's feeling for the natural world already evident in her observations of Shanghai, but St. Andrews offered an education of another kind. The town had been founded in the 1780s, and still retains impressive examples of Georgian and Neo-classical architecture. These buildings' elegant symmetry, simple massing, pleasing proportions, and classical details such as pediments over doorways, windows framed by cornice and pilasters, and decorative transom windows, offered a distinctive aesthetic education.[21] Where Shanghai was characterised by continual shift and transience, St. Andrews must have embodied solidity and permanence.

In Shanghai as a child she lived in the garden (a poignant echo of traditional Chinese upper-class female seclusion). In New Brunswick she could clamber below rocky sea cliffs, roam along headlands and through stands of maple, spruce and balsam, and watch the famous Fundy tide rushing into the Passamaquoddy Bay. This same fierce, clawing tide had uncovered fossils that were intimating just how ancient the local landscape was. In 1851 fossilised tree trunks and the tiny bones of the world's first reptiles were discovered in cliff faces at the head of the Bay of Fundy. Maybe Florence with her younger brothers Geoffrey and Gordon combed along stretches of rocky coast, hunting for agates, amethyst, jasper and the fossils of sea creatures. Maybe she held the Coal Age fossil of a lobe-finned fish in her palm, or peered at the tracks of early amphibians and comprehended a folding back of time. And in that comprehension of hundreds of millions of years, she might easily grasp the notion of China's 5,000 years of human civilization.

It is also possible that during those childhood years of shuttling between Shanghai and St. Andrews she first absorbed the Daoist philosophical concept of the complements *yin* and *yang* that she later so often explained to a Western audience. St. Andrews—*yang* in its bedrock and northern clear sunlight. Shanghai—*yin* in its yielding soft sandiness and fugitive southern cityscape.

When Thomas Wheelock brought his family to Boston in 1889, there is every indication that the Chinese episode of their lives was concluded. However in 1897, the family's first year at Topside, Wheelock had to return to China for the winter. The reason was a leave of absence taken by Frank Gove, who was managing part of the Wheelock businesses.[22] Gove appears to have belonged to the New Brunswick family into which Thomas's sister Isabella married; he had worked for Wheelock and Company since the early 1880s, according to the *Desk Hong* directories. To cover his absence Wheelock returned to Shanghai accompanied by his wife and daughter, while Geoffrey and Gordon remained in America. Geoffrey was attending Harvard, from where he graduated in 1901. The pages of the student newspaper *The Harvard Crimson* chart his prowess on the golf links and exploits on the football field. He may have been an even more expert golfer than his father; in 1901 he merited a mention in *The New York Times* as the Harvard Golf Champion.[23] His younger brother followed him to Harvard in 1901 but died in his freshman year in April 1902, from an acute attack of bronchitis following measles.[24] Florence never mentions Gordon in her books, possibly in reaction to the doubtless painful shock of losing her brother so suddenly as a young man.

When Thomas, Edith and Florence Wheelock returned to China they were temporarily homeless, and stayed with friends in the bustling quarters of a *hong*—a walled compound consisting of a firm's business premises, warehouses, and living quarters for the foreign staff. By the end of the nineteenth century this arrangement, though convivial, was already passé. The mansion on Bubbling Well Road had probably been sold before the family left for Boston. Appositely in light of Ayscough's career, the site became the clubhouse for the International Recreation Club, founded in 1908 by Ye Ziheng in response to his exclusion from the Shanghai Race Club, whose elected chairmen and members were drawn almost exclusively from the ranks of the British upper class. When Ayscough re-visited Shanghai in 1927, the house, but not its gardens, still existed, but in 1929 it was replaced by a handsome new clubhouse designed by Palmer and Turner. The International Recreation Club welcomed both Chinese and foreigners, and aimed to facilitate interaction between nationalities—a goal with which Ayscough would become profoundly allied.

From their friend's *hong*, the Wheelocks moved back to the familiar territory of the Bund. Had she been able to spare the time, Florence would have spent mesmeric days with her nose pressed against the flat's windowpanes, gazing at the brown-sailed junks manned by crews dressed in country indigo, the flotillas of cargo boats, the ever present warships, and the sampans 'which looked like little cockleshells dancing on the swiftly flowing river, their scarlet prows sharply upturned and their white-lacquered hoods shining in the sun'.[25] The fact though, was that this was the active rather than contemplative phase of Ayscough's life; she was simply too absorbed in the daily round of lunching, dining and dancing. The days of trotting around the garden led by her groom were over; now, like her father, she was a keen cross-country rider and cantered across the Shanghai countryside on a white pony given to her by her father as a Christmas present. This countryside was expansive, though hardly unpopulated; hard-riding foreign equestrians received regular warnings about destroying plots of wheat and barley, and churning up grave mounds when the ground was sodden. In a photograph from around this time she stands square, with whip and pistol, wasp-waisted from vigorous exercise, and possibly corsetry (*Figure 3*).

As a wealthy young woman of marriageable age, she now participated in the upper echelons of Shanghai's social circuit and its multifarious opportunities for sport and recreation. One memorable costume ball was hosted by a group of bachelors who called themselves The Four and Twenty Blackbirds. Edith Wheelock went dressed as a bottle of champagne, in a green satin dress with a gold bodice, and white powdered hair representing the foam. Florence

Figure 3 Florence Wheelock Ayscough, Shanghai Dec. 1899. Special Collections, Armacost Library, University of Redlands.

went as a member of a group of four young women and four men, dressed as queens and knaves.

None of the four knaves became suitors, but at another dinner party she sat beside a more promising tall Englishman, whom she induced to accompany her to the walled Chinese City, the nest-shaped nucleus of Shanghai's ancient city. By the time Eva Dunlap created her map in the 1930s, the walls had been partially demolished, though the district was still girdled by gates. When Ayscough first visited though, the city walls were crumbling, but they still represented a physical and psychological barrier between the native and foreign-controlled districts. In 1899 the redoubtably well-travelled explorer Isabella Bird contrasted the cloying density and ceaseless din of 'this native hive' with the broad, light-filled and well-swept avenues of foreign Shanghai, concluding that it was little surprise so few foreigners ventured into an enclave in which it was 'bad form to show any interest'.[26]

Missionaries had generally been the native city's most regular foreign visitors, but by the late nineteenth century it had become fashionable among a subculture of adventurous spirits to penetrate beyond the walls. Generally, Western visitors were squeamishly fascinated with the odours, squalor, and openly displayed deformities of beggars. In 1900 the American photographer and geographer Eliza Scidmore (the first woman to serve on the board of managers of the National Geographic Society) documented a visit in which she was pursued by a woman juggler with bound feet after she responded inadequately to an acrobatic act involving the somersaulting of a thin, pale child.[27]

Even as late as 1916, although it was only a ten-cent rickshaw ride to the city gates, few foreigners made the trip—which was a great pity, as they also missed the melancholic and deserted gardens with their water lily ponds, blowsy hollyhocks going to seed, and grass pushing between the steps. By the time of Eva Dunlap's map two decades later, the Chinese City had become a fairly standard excursion, though guidebooks recommended the services of a reputable guide.

Ayscough's response in 1898 was predictably visceral. She recoiled from the press of humanity in the narrow alleys, noisome air, and cobbles slick with filth. The beggars crying piteously for charity especially distressed her. Later, though, the Old City became one of her important sources of knowledge. There was the Yu Garden, where she would study the aesthetics of Chinese garden design. The City God Temple became one of her favourite haunts where she would observe the intermingling of Daoism, Buddhism and popular religion played out before her in prayer and pageantry.

There was the Confucian temple where she would contemplate the other great system of thought that had shaped Chinese society. She studied these places as a historian and ethnographer, and her later writings on these go far beyond travelogues—she grasps philosophical systems far removed from anything in the experience of most Western readers and presents them in a way that is intellectually accessible, as well as enjoyable. She shares her own pleasure in the sensory details of these places: the gorgeously dressed children accompanying parents to worship, the fall of light through mother of pearl panes onto beaten lead 'spirit money', the seal cutters and fortune tellers and vendors of toothsome snacks.

She came to understand that begging was an organized trade in Shanghai, with its own complex structures—guilds even—and systems of fees for shops wishing to avoid beggars' imprecations. But back in 1898 she was so tormented by the memory of one particularly unfortunate old woman that she induced her companion to return the next day with money.

That companion was Francis Ayscough (1859–1933), who was soon to become her husband. And this first act of magnanimity set in course over three decades of devotion until his death. Scattered throughout her correspondence would be references to him waiting overnight on station platforms, or forced to hang around for days on end in Japan for a missed ocean liner. Francis Ayscough was a British businessman, son of Ethel Fearon and Thomas Ayscough, the scholarly Rector of St. James the Great, Cradley, Herefordshire.[28] Francis had grown up in the luxuriantly beautiful and fertile countryside of the Malvern Hills, surrounded by Tudor half-timbered architecture. His father's church was Norman and fifteenth-century, with Victorian additions by Sir Gilbert Scott. His childhood home was a gracious Georgian brick rectory. From such beginnings, it is no surprise that Francis Ayscough should devote much of his leisure time as an adult to recreating beauty. Francis had been educated at Winchester, and according to one source, had come to Shanghai in 1882.[29] He doesn't appear in the *Desk Hong* directories, though, until 1891, as an employee of Turnbull, Howie and Co., which later became Scott, Harding and Co. Its business was initially the export of tea and silk, but during Ayscough's tenure it focused increasingly on import, and added an engineering department. A successful businessman, Francis Ayscough was also firmly entrenched in the administrative apparatus of the International Settlement. During his at least three decade sojourn in the city he served on the Shanghai Municipal Council (the administrative body charged with managing the affairs of the International Settlement), the Parks Committee and was Chairman of the Shanghai Gas Company (the public utility responsible for providing gas to the Settlement), as well as of several prominent social and commercial organizations.

Francis Ayscough and Florence Wheelock married at Trinity Church Boston on 23 December 1898.[30] Although Ayscough was sixteen years older than his bride, they shared much in common. Both came from families that valued education. Now in China, apart from a solidly established British Shanghailander identity, their most obvious tie was a love of sports, particularly horse-riding. During the 1890s, Francis Ayscough appeared frequently in the pages of the *North China Herald* for his hunting prowess. In 1890 he was elected a steward of the Paper Hunt Club, served as Secretary from 1890 to 1897, then as Master until 1898.[31] A peculiarly British colonial pastime, the Paper Hunt involved a rider, acting as 'prey' laying a paper trail ahead of the pack. In Shanghai it was played on stocky Mongolian ponies from November to March around the outlying countryside when theoretically the fields were fallow, though there is plenty of evidence that careless riders damaged peasants' property and grave mounds.

Francis Ayscough seems to have been as vigorous as his young wife, if *Social Shanghai* is to be believed. The magazine claimed of the sturdy ponies, 'They can jump like cats and have no end of pluck, and the last remark may also be applied to many of the riders.'[32] Hunts tended to conclude with sweating ponies smothered in dust, their riders having swallowed great quantities of it too. At the end of the final hunt of the 1898 season a parched and exhausted Francis Ayscough is quoted in the *North China Herald*: 'the hunt has been a very fast and furious one, and it has taken what little oratorical power I possess out of me.'[33] He was more gallantly eloquent at the Club's Annual General Meeting that November, conceding that he was relinquishing his position because of his upcoming marriage. Whereas Florence remembered a dinner party and an excursion to the Old City, Francis remembered canters, and exhilarating leaps over brooks and fences: 'Had it not been for cross-country-riding I should possibly not have made the acquaintance of my fiancée, and on that account I feel that I owe cross-country riding a very heartfelt debt of gratitude.'[34] At the closing of the season the Paper Hunt Races took place at the Race Course, attended by 'nearly all residents of any importance'. Each year the finely dressed spectators certainly included the Ayscoughs.

The grounds of the Race Course on Bubbling Well Road, not far from Florence's childhood home, were significant for all members of her family. Horse racing was endemic to Empire; almost all important British colonial cities were endowed with race tracks. Shanghai had its own racetrack just a few years after the Treaty of Nanking (1842), though the final expanded track was laid out later, in 1862. Francis was a steward at this most exclusive club, whose membership was drawn largely from elite British Shanghailanders.

Outside the May and November racing seasons, the clubhouse and grounds inside the racetrack were used for other sporting and social occasions. A nine-hole golf course was laid out and the Shanghai Golf Club established in 1894. It wasn't until 1912 that an 18-hole course was laid out at Kiangwan (Jiangwan), in the northern suburbs. When Thomas Wheelock left his spacious, windswept links behind in St. Andrews, New Brunswick, Shanghai's modest course on the recreation grounds allowed him to resume his passion. When his son Geoffrey returned to Shanghai to become a partner in Wheelock and Co., and then Director of the Shanghai Tug and Lighter Co., predictably he too continued to play golf. He was President of the Golf Club in the first decade of the twentieth century, and there was even a Wheelock Cup. His sister too participated in this favourite family sport; Florence was on the organizing committee for the Shanghai Ladies' Golf Club in 1902. She became well enough acquainted with the greenkeeper at Qingdao (which became a popular northern resort once it was leased to Germany prior to the First World War) that he gave her a scroll of calligraphy as a parting gift. The Shanghai Recreation Ground was also the venue for a variety of less serious and traditional pursuits with which the Wheelocks and Ayscoughs have no recorded connection. The more fatuous include a gymkhana for cars hosted by the Automobile Club, comprised of games such as a variant of musical chairs in which ladies leapt from cars and raced for vacant chairs.[35]

With Francis, Florence entered a compatible and comfortable marriage that cemented her Shanghailander identity. She enjoyed the wealth, leisure and stability that allowed her to cultivate her interests and to travel. Three 'line-a-day' diaries survive from her

Shanghai years; the entries are, obviously, condensed, but they do present a picture of an energetic, sociable woman who played golf and tennis, yachted, walked, and enjoyed the company of many friends.[36] A consideration of some of the couple's mutual interests contributes to an understanding of family life for Westerners in Concession-era Shanghai. Their closeness counters the popular notion that lifestyles were polarized according to gender, with the men absorbed in business, then in their clubs, while their wives shopped and lunched.

On returning to Shanghai, the Ayscoughs' first necessity was to find a home. The *hong* where Francis had been living as a bachelor had been sold, and the couple faced the difficulty that has been a constant feature of Shanghai life for all its residents—securing appropriate dwelling space in a heavily congested, circumscribed area subject to constant real estate speculation and shortage of supply. They chose the usual solution, and moved further out of town, relying on a recalcitrant former race pony to draw their carriage. The boundaries of the International Settlement were formally extended to both the west and the north in 1899, requiring improvements in transportation. A plan to introduce trams was floated in the 1890s and Florence, ever-keen on technology, was a keen supporter, but found herself pitted against reactionary opinion (it wasn't until 1908 that a tram network opened). At a huge race club tiffin (luncheon) she found herself arguing with a respected director of a large *hong*, and member of the Shanghai Municipal Council. Engrossed in her argument, she was horrified to hear herself declare, against a backdrop of a silent table of twenty five persons, 'You might just as well have come out of the ark!'[37] It was a foretaste of the strong-mindedness that would later pit her against some of the West's most acclaimed translators of Chinese poetry.

In 1900 Florence's address was listed in the city directory as 25 Sinza Road (now Xinzha Road), in what were then the far western suburbs. Eva Dunlap has depicted a gracious Dutch-gabled villa on the site, but 35 years previously the area had been rather remote, accessed by a bridge over a creek. With usual good humour Ayscough christened her small rental 'The Moated Grange'.

The next year her father proposed that he build them their own house. They chose a large plot of land some distance from the centre of Shanghai, but still within the boundaries of the International Settlement, on a northern stretch of Gordon Road (now Jiangning Road). This was also eventually to be the site of the Grass Hut, which they built much later. One of the reasons for this choice was that here, on the edge of the Settlement where land was more plentiful they could create a large garden. Both Francis and Florence were to become passionate gardeners and important figures in Shanghai's horticultural scene (one example of a shared ground in which foreigners and Chinese genuinely interacted to mutual benefit). And as a manifestation of Chinese culture, Chinese garden aesthetics came to be one of Florence's major preoccupations, and another means of expressing the union of the active and contemplative aspects of her nature.

In 1901–2, however, the couple's imagination did not reach beyond the construction of a large, stylistically Western structure, that reminded a friend of Bar Harbor, Maine. In his autobiography, J. G. Ballard, born later but not far from the Grass Hut, noted that each nationality in Shanghai built houses modelled on the ones of their homelands. Photographs of the Ayscoughs' house soon after its completion depict a large three-storey structure whose prominent feature is a wrap-around open veranda that extends over the three floors.[38] Certainly it was reminiscent of the summer homes of east-coast America; it was also a practical architectural response to Shanghai's hot and humid summers. The gardens are as yet unplanted in early photographs, though the grounds appear vast and savannah-like. In one 1903 photograph Florence, Francis and her father sit in what was likely to have been this garden with a set tea table, potted chrysanthemums and the dogs Moses and Aaron. She is beaming (*Figure 4*).

Initially the couple considered calling their new home The Hall of Purple Delights, but reconsidered, and named it Wild Goose Happiness House. In its extensive gardens the Ayscoughs were to hold parties and fund-raisers, and to grow the flowers and vegetables that were to win both of them many prizes at the Shanghai Horticultural Society's shows. The property was surrounded by

Figure 4 Frank Ayscough, Florence, Tom Wheelock, Moses and Aaron, 1903. Special Collections, Armacost Library, University of Redlands.

a high bamboo fence and guarded by a Sikh watchman who was a long-time family servant. On several occasions they were the victims of petty crime, the most serious perpetrated by a thief who was brought to trial for assaulting the watchman Gala Singh.[39] The *North China Herald* commented that such incidents against the foreign community were commonplace, though rarely reported— a foretaste of the more virulent anti-foreigner sentiment noted by journalist Agnes Smedley in the early 1930s when she observed how shocked the Westerners were at the chalked slogans on the walls of their lovely gardens urging 'Down with the Imperialists!'.

Although still within the International Settlement (if only just), the Ayscoughs' new home existed within a highly traditional, self-contained 'village'—an arrangement that was typical for the ordinary Chinese residents who comprised the majority of the Settlement's inhabitants. Dunlap's map, like all cartography, tells a truth particular to the maker or those for whom the map is made. English-language maps of Shanghai tend to emphasize the commercial thoroughfares, landmarks and recreational areas that made up a Western *idea* of the city. A Chinese resident living in a lane house could access services, stores, work, leisure, all within a few neighbourhood blocks. He might visit a 'major' artery such as Nanjing Road only once or twice in his life.[40] The neighbourhood around Wild Goose Happiness House was the relevant Shanghai for the local Chinese who lived there, and it would have given Florence Ayscough an alternate experience of her city.

Fragments at least of traditional architecture survived. Although like similar outlying areas it experienced influxes of migrants, it had traditionally been inhabited by the Yang clan, who had been honoured by the erection of a memorial arch which was now the focus of village life: 'Old people sat by it sunning themselves, children brought their crickets in little cages to sing in its shadow …'[41] Mores and customs were changing, but according to Ayscough the residents took an implicit satisfaction in their village's rootedness in the traditional Confucian code. The arch commemorated a widow of the Yang family who remained chaste after her husband's death.

Over the years of the Ayscoughs' residence the surrounding area became heavily industrialized, but at first there were plots of winter and summer wheat, rape, cotton and peach trees. With her *lo-sze* pug Yo Fei, she daily walked to nearby Suzhou Creek, and took the ferry across to the open fields and villages beyond, where she observed kite festivals and funerals and the wealth of intangible culture that she would use in her writings and illustrated lectures. At least physically, she inhabited both worlds, striding through the countryside in the morning, then in the afternoon slipping into the world of increasingly cosmopolitan and modern Shanghai depicted in Dunlap's map.

A little south of their home was 28 Connaught Road, where the Shanghai Gun Club, established in 1895, was headquartered. As wife of the Club's President, it was often Florence's privilege to present the cup to the day's best shot—sometimes her husband! She conducted this duty with the requisite good form, as the *North China Herald* approvingly recorded in June 1908: '… in a few pleasant words [she] congratulated the winners and complimented them on their good scores'.[42] Photographed in *Social Shanghai* she smiles graciously at a prizewinner (*Figure 5*). She may have enjoyed this sport herself, but at the Gun Club she joined other dutiful spectator wives, standing in Shanghai's soaking rains and wilting heat. The *North China Herald* noted that their support was, however, acknowledged: 'At the conclusion of the proceedings three cheers were given for the ladies who, notwithstanding the weather, assembled to witness the shooting.'[43] Whatever her private

Figure 5 Florence Ayscough presenting the winner's cup at Shanghai Gun Club, 1912, *Social Shanghai*.

inclination at this time, her second husband noted that she became a member of the Society for the Prevention of Cruelty to Animals, expressed concern for the solicitous treatment of caged chickens, and disliked meat.

Geoffrey Wheelock made his home nearby at 16 Connaught Road. He had married Mary Wendell, who was a daughter of Barrett Wendell, Professor of English at Harvard University and a correspondent of Amy Lowell. Geoffrey was also a member of the Gun Club as well as several other sports clubs, and as with his father and brother-in-law, the Shanghai newspapers regularly documented his sporting prowess at these venues.

The Gun Club was acknowledged as an important Shanghailander social as well as sporting institution. The other club most infamous for its male British exclusivity (and, interestingly, omitted from Dunlap's map) was the Shanghai Club. Both Francis and Geoffrey were members. Florence had another familial link to this building at No. 2, The Bund. Opened in 1864 and brought into a state of financial ruin by prodigality and poor management, it had been auctioned off by Wheelock and Co. in 1870.

While Florence was excluded by gender from belonging to the Shanghai Club (though she probably attended balls there), she did belong to the Country Club on Bubbling Well Road. Another largely British institution, it excluded Jews and Chinese from its gracious gardens, swimming pool, tennis courts and well-equipped clubhouse. The existence of such institutions is an undeniable fact of Concession-era Shanghai, which operated as a matter of fact on exclusion. Some foreigners, such as the leftist writer Agnes Smedley, remonstrated through personally boycotting the Country Club. As part of the ruling apparatus of the Settlement, the Ayscoughs seem to have accepted the structures by which it operated. Florence had many Chinese friends and later colleagues; she was to build her career on the interpretation of Chinese culture—be it poetry, art, or horticulture. That the people who owned that culture were not permitted into certain clubs or onto the Shanghai Municipal Council until 1928 was not a subject Ayscough initially addressed. Politically reticent, she only dropped oblique clues about her alignments and beliefs in her books. It was only in her later career—particularly during her second marriage to the China foreign policy specialist Harley MacNair, after Francis' tragic death, that she was to become more publicly outspoken on matters political and discriminatory.

Francis Ayscough served as Chairman of the Country Club in 1920. The couple enjoyed its social benefits, but Florence was also to find an audience there. In February she delivered a lecture on Chinese culture, and the proceeds were donated to the British

Women's Work Association, an organization founded to assist British soldiers during the First World War. This raises another important facet of Shanghailander life, particularly for women—philanthropy. In a city with such gross extremes of wealth and poverty, the alleviation of suffering was considered by many as a moral imperative. Throughout her life Florence volunteered her time to charities, often selecting those which assisted women. Among other activities she served on the board of a refuge for girls in Shanghai. Several of these operated in the city, some being affiliated to religious institutions, and their work was often publicized in English-language newspapers, or through lectures. Although insulated through status, Florence would have been well aware of the miseries of young children who were abused as household slaves, or sold into prostitution. She shared such concerns with many wealthy foreign women, including the wife of the Governor of Hong Kong, Lady Lugard, as well as many missionary women. Such philanthropic efforts towards an unsavoury subject may have been spurred by a desire to exhibit independence of spirit; in Ayscough's case they were probably motivated more by a realization that child slavery was a blatant aspect of life in the metropolis. Realities interweave: on the same day in February 1917 that Ayscough urges her elite audience at the Country Club to 'see into the lives' of local Shanghainese, Miss Laura White lectures on the rising epidemic of prostitution to members of the Women's Christian Temperance Union in the Union Church Hall.[44]

During the First World War Ayscough was described as 'an ardent worker' for the British Women's Work Association, along with her brother's wife Mary Wheelock, who also created an organization to aid indigent Chinese women. Both assisted with the necessary but bleak work of securing the vast quantities of bandages and shrouds needed for the army. She gave her efforts to famine relief in provinces that were routinely shattered by poor harvests or civil strife. She fully understood that in provinces neighbouring wealthy Shanghai could be found Chinese starving to death in their homes.

Among the many tributes published after Ayscough's death, several attested to her generosity in helping small local causes, or the often invisible work of enriching the lives of children. The Ayscoughs were childless; none of her extant letters alludes to any particular reason. They had a nephew in 1904, born to Geoffrey and Mary—Thomas Gordon Wheelock (named after Florence and Geoffrey's deceased younger brother).[45] She seems, though, to have had an empathy with children that expressed itself through acts of generosity. For instance, when Anna Pavlova danced in Shanghai in 1922, Ayscough paid for a private performance for Shanghai schoolchildren.

For a city decried as crassly commercial, the Shanghai of Dunlap's map offered plenty of cultural opportunities to those who looked for them, whether a ballet performance by Pavlova, a Schubert concert, or an exhibition of classical Chinese paintings. There was the American Women's Club, to which Ayscough lectured on Amy Lowell. This had started as a literary society, but during Ayscough's residence in Shanghai held a vibrant programme of cultural activities such as visits to notable private arts collections—including Ayscough's own. The Shanghai Art Club on Avenue Joffre (now Huaihai Road), which supported local artists and exhibited work, was an important meeting ground for both Ayscough and Dunlap. During most of Ayscough's time in Shanghai the Town Hall was situated on Nanking Road. It was used by the Shanghai Horticultural Society for many of their annual shows—here Francis judged, and Florence so often won.

The Shanghai Philharmonic, in which Florence played first violin, performed Schumann and Mendelssohn at the Town Hall.

And, most importantly for this story, the North China Branch of the Royal Asiatic Society was housed on Museum Road (now Huqiu Road), just behind the Bund. A British Foreign Office official called it flatteringly, though not entirely accurately, 'the one bright spot in Shanghai'.[46] Ayscough's Shanghai was full of moment, inspiration and illumination, but she credited the Royal Asiatic Society for providing the intellectual foundation to her life's work as a translator of Chinese culture.

2
Images
The Tastemaker

There are many reasons for learning, or not learning, a foreign language; Florence Ayscough may be the only Westerner who learnt Chinese out of politeness.

Most Shanghailanders didn't speak any Chinese. From their perspective, there was no necessity. Their household staff spoke pidgin, and compradors eased communication between foreign businessmen and the Chinese people. Cultural prejudice disinclined most Western settlers from learning the language of a semi-colonised people. Besides, there was no standard Chinese language until the twentieth century, and most Chinese spoke a regional dialect. Missionaries might become fluent, especially those isolated from their compatriots; administrators or certain government employees such as municipal police officers might be required to attain some command of Chinese; sinologists sank themselves into decoding the written form of literary Chinese. But Shanghailanders of the Ayscoughs' position were apt to look with distrust on any of their peers studying Chinese for pleasure. Florence's second husband Harley MacNair pointed out just how extraordinary it was for Ayscough to become enthralled with Chinese when, 'Everything in Shanghai, except its location, militated against this:

her family duties and her position, the snobbishly compartmentalized social life of international Shanghai, the Chinese general attitude toward Westerners and that of the majority of Westerners toward the Chinese.'[1] An episode in W. Somerset Maugham's 1922 irreverent collection of sketches *On a Chinese Screen* might be thought to parody the 'treaty port people' whose dinner party talk is of racing, golf and shooting, and any person learning Chinese considered 'queer in the head'; except that Florence Ayscough met the same consternation among her friends when she proposed her own plans. 'Oh I wouldn't! Jenks studied the language and soon went mad!' she was warned.

Like a 'sheep', she admits, she let the matter lie, until the blistering summer of 1905, when she was visited by a family friend, Mark Napier Trollope, who would become the Anglican Bishop of Korea, and President of the Korea Branch of the Royal Asiatic Society. In the humidity Trollope was made miserable by his self-imposed sartorial propriety. After several days she induced him to change into cooler attire, but was still disconcerted by his melancholia. She confesses that she embarked then on 'the stony path of Chinese learning' in an effort to distract her guest from his brooding, through asking him to teach her to use his pocket Chinese dictionary. After he returned to England she grappled with the dictionary alone for several more years.

The world-weary foreigners of Maugham's treaty port are bored with China and with each other. The Hongkong and Shanghai Bank manager and the 'number one at Jardine's' have seen each daily for too many years to have anything of interest left to say. Florence Ayscough, however, was never boring or bored. She moved easily through diplomatic and business circles, and counted as close friends figures such as Sir Pelham Warren, the British Consul General in Shanghai, Sir Havilland de Sausmarez, the Judge of the British Supreme Court for China, and John C. Ferguson, educator, government advisor, newspaper proprietor and art expert. Such friendships were to offer an entrée into an unexpectedly expansive new world.

Florence's awakening interest in Chinese culture led her in 1906 to the library of the Royal Asiatic Society. Established in 1857 as a learned society (and to alleviate what was often perceived as an intellectually barren, overly commercially obsessed society), the North China Branch of the Royal Asiatic Society could count many achievements over the intervening half century; it produced a lecture series, published a highly respected journal, encouraged the learning of the Chinese language, and was building up an impressive library. Although not yet a member of the Society, Ayscough borrowed several valuable books that she then had trouble returning, as library hours were unpredictable. She confessed her embarrassment over dinner with the Society's Honorary Secretary, John C. Ferguson. She recalls in *Firecracker Land* the impact this discussion was to have on her life:

> He [Ferguson] talked at length about books, about
> the library, about Chinese matters in general, and
> about the difficulties of administering the library in
> particular, and I parted from him feeling my already
> keen interest a thousand times keener. I determined
> to join the society and read everything possible about
> China.[3]

Several days later Sir Pelham Warren, President of the Society and already a close friend, informed her that the council was offering her the position of Honorary Librarian and the daunting task of re-cataloguing the library—a profession she protested she knew nothing about. Warren's response, she recollected was, 'Neither do any of us, and you have more time to learn than we have!'

It was not in spite of but *because* of the opportunities that existed in this mercantile city, and because of the people who lived there, and because of Shanghai's physical and cultural environment that Ayscough was able to develop as a scholar. Over-emphasis on Shanghai's cultural deficiencies overlooks the Chinese aspect of its historical development.

Until the second half of the nineteenth century Shanghai had been far eclipsed as a centre of culture and learning by the other Jiangnan cities of Hangzhou, Suzhou and Yangzhou. The Taiping Rebellion and the prolonged civil unrest in the region eventually unseated these cities, as scholars, scientists, wealthy merchants and collectors migrated to Shanghai, which remained relatively safe from civil strife. Shanghai, at first as refuge for intellectuals and entrepreneurs, assumed a position as a centre for advanced scientific thinking and cultural exchange. For example, the migration to Shanghai of Chinese scholars Li Shanlan and Wang Tao resulted in their groundbreaking scientific translations with the British missionary Alexander Wylie, who had amassed a large library of Chinese and English books. Some of these were sold to the North China Branch of the Royal Asiatic Society and formed the core of the library for which Ayscough was to become guardian.

In 1897, the year the Wheelocks returned to Shanghai, a group of four young Chinese men opened a printing press on a corner of Kiangse Road (now Jiangxi Road). The Commercial Press became Shanghai's dominant publishing house, and was to play a significant role in the transformation of Shanghai into a modern centre of East–West cultural exchange. Working with eminent China scholars, it produced compilations of classical Chinese literature and new editions of rare books (vitally important at a time when precious historical manuscripts were being purchased by overseas buyers and lost to China). It translated Western scientific and literary texts, and published a widely used Chinese–English dictionary. It also established its own library, at its height containing over half a million books, many of them rare and irreplaceable. The loss of this library in the Japanese bombing of the city in 1932 during the First Shanghai War was a catastrophe for bibliophiles. The private library that Florence Ayscough was to build (and later donate to the US Library of Congress) contained many books published by the Commercial Press. One of her own titles, a bibliography of general-interest books on China, was published by the Press in 1921 as were several books by her second husband, Harley MacNair.[4]

For those who chose to become engaged, to be in Shanghai at the start of the twentieth century was to be in a context of fervid cultural exchange. Foreign sojourners and tourists produced a steady stream of travelogue, scholarship, journalism and fiction about China; the Chinese were hungry for Western medical and scientific expertise, and were additionally mining their own past to rediscover and reinterpret classic literature and philosophy—which then became available to Western scholars. Shanghai became a knowledge arsenal. A driving force of this accumulation of knowledge had been China's Self-Strengthening Movement during the previous decades. The origins of this movement, in the early 1860s, lay in the acknowledgement of the decline of the Qing dynasty, as evinced by military defeats and concessions to foreign powers. Widescale reforms aimed at arresting this decline focused on the acquisition of Western technical and scientific knowledge, and modern armaments, as well as an overhaul of commerce, industry and agriculture (though not of political systems and social structures). A major site of this activity was the Jiangnan Arsenal in Shanghai, the largest arsenal in East Asia. From 1868 to 1912 it ran a translation department producing Chinese translations of

Western scientific literature and international news. One of the instructors was the aforementioned missionary-scholar Alexander Wylie. The library of the Royal Asiatic Society, far from being 'the one bright spot in Shanghai', was rather one cog in the wheel of a giant machine producing and disseminating knowledge in this very particular place and time.

To be in Shanghai at the start of the twentieth century was also, unavoidably, to be in a climate of surging Chinese nationalism. The decades the Wheelocks spent in China saw the aftermath of the Treaty of Nanking, the slow disintegration of the Qing empire, and (while the Wheelocks were back in Boston) the humiliation of a defeat by Japan in 1895 in the first Sino-Japanese War. Anti-Qing revolutionaries, nationalists fomenting for the ejection of foreigners, and proto-communists found common ground in Shanghai. The threat of violence from the virulently anti-imperialist Boxer Rebellion hung over the city at the turn of the century, as the family would soon discover. The Jiangnan Arsenal was an asset of the late Qing empire, but unofficial arsenals were being created in Shanghai's quiet *lilongs* of compact lane housing not far from the residences of foreign company directors, Settlement administrators, and the barracks of Municipal policemen. In 1906, the year Florence Ayscough joined the Royal Asiatic Society, the young woman revolutionary Qiu Jin began making bombs in Hongkou, not far to the east of the Ayscoughs' home.

So many unlikely correspondences: Qiu Jin had been born in 1875, the same year as Ayscough; as a child she rode horses, as a young woman she wrote poetry (subsequently translated by Ayscough); much later, her daughter lived very close to Ayscough, and related stories of her mother, whose life story had completely captivated the writer. All of this, including Ayscough's later book on Chinese women which shared Qiu Jin's story with a Western readership, lay far in the future. But 1907, the year Ayscough became the Society's librarian, and the year Qiu Jin, just 31 years of age, was publicly beheaded, was a watershed.

This young woman, whose unconventional acquisition of Chinese had been so *ad hoc*, could now, through books, touch the minds of great scholars. When she resigned her post as librarian in 1922 she reflected, 'I feel that through the doors of its library, I have been enabled to enter another world—a world in which the boundaries of time and space often seem annihilated. It has been my endeavour to hold open this door that others might enter.'[5]

At first she catalogued, and what might have seemed a dry and daunting task was instead a period of discovery and wonder. Through her hands passed the seminal work of notable sinologists (many of them Society members) such as Paul Pelliot, James Legge, Robert Morrison, H. A. Giles and Alexander Wylie. Astonishingly, given the vicissitudes and destructions of the past century, the books Ayscough handled are still together, safe in a former Jesuit library now owned by the Shanghai Library. It is possible to pore over them, as Ayscough did, in a quiet reading room that obliterates the distance between now and then. In her 1909 catalogue are the books that must have distracted her from her preliminary task: the Jesuits' *Lettres Edifiantes et Curieuses*; *The Typhoons of the Chinese Seas*; *European Botanical Discoveries in China*; *Bird of the Lower Yang-tse Basin*; *Hospital Dialogue in Mandarin*; *My Diary in a Chinese Farm*; *Rambles Round Shanghai*; *A Summer Ride through Western Thibet*.

Scrawled notes one hundred years old, spider-scratch attempts to write Chinese characters, an envelope addressed with the old French Concession street name, Route Doumer, slipped between pages as a bookmark and forgotten. These fall from the pages of books that were handled by Ayscough, her assistants and successors. These books sat on bedside tables on Rue Lafayette and Avenue Pétain; they were read in the gardens of Route Père Robert and Lucerne Road; they were packed up in trunks and taken with the children to the summer resorts of Moganshan and Weihaiwei. Their borrowers' names are recorded on the slips still tucked into holders on the backboards. In these small discursions history is very close and literally palpable.

In the old Society building on Museum Road, while the termites chewed and chewed, Florence browsed and read, assimilating the scholarship of Society members and sinologists. She attended the lectures that were deemed monuments of erudition. Increasingly, she became fascinated by Chinese art, and especially the interactions between painting and calligraphy. In these pursuits she was encouraged by her friend, the Society's Honorary Secretary and journal editor John C. Ferguson (1865–1945), who had originally come to China as a Methodist missionary in 1887. Ferguson was one of the rare *passepartout* occasionally encountered among sojourners from overseas. Canadian-born and educated in the United States, he was multi-talented, multilingual, sophisticated and indefatigable. He left his missionary post in 1897, and completed a Ph.D., writing his thesis on *The Confucian Renaissance in the Sung Dynasty*. He developed an impressive career as an educator and government advisor, forging friendships and alliances with Chinese intellectuals, high-ranking politicians and members of both the Qing and Republican social elite. Simultaneously, he developed an expertise in Chinese art that was to enable him to collect for major American institutions such as the Metropolitan Museum of Art, and the Freer Gallery of Art. As a friend, colleague and mentor, Ferguson undoubtedly had an impact on Ayscough's own connoisseurship, helping her develop her own connections with Chinese collectors and, in time, major American art museums.

The first of their shared enterprises was an event that has now been almost entirely forgotten, but at the time made the bedazzling claim to be China's first art exhibition. Held in November 1908 in the Shanghai Mutual Telephone Company Building on Kiangse Road, the event was organized by the Royal Asiatic Society partly as a fund-raiser for the library.[6] More importantly in professional and social terms, it brought together prestigious Chinese and Western collectors and established the Society's credibility with an art-appreciating audience far beyond the boundaries of Shanghai. The driving force behind this exhibition of 3,000 pieces of porcelain, glass, jade, lacquer and ivory was Abel W. Bahr. Like Ayscough he had been born in Shanghai, in 1877, but to a Chinese mother and German father. Like Ferguson he was fluent in Chinese, and counted many prominent Chinese among his friends. A collector of Chinese porcelain since 1905, he would shortly leave Shanghai in 1910 to pursue a successful career as an art dealer in Britain.

The connections of both Bahr and Ferguson helped the Society secure the assistance of Chinese government officials who served on the organizing committee or loaned art. Ferguson used his diplomatic connections to secure items from prominent Chinese collectors such as the governor Duanfang (1861–1911), a high-ranking Qing official who lent important Song-dynasty burial ware, among other exhibits. Sadly, his negotiations of loans from the imperial collections were disrupted by the deaths of both the Guangxu Emperor and Empress Dowager Cixi in 1908.

The majority of the works on display were Ming- and Qing-dynasty ceramics reflecting the tastes of both Western and Chinese collectors of the period.[7] Among these collectors was Florence Ayscough. By 1908 she had been a member of the Society for only two years, yet she served on a committee that included Ferguson, Warren, Bahr, and Chinese officials. Bahr claimed that all committee members were 'well known in Shanghai as connoisseurs', and during the opening ceremony Ayscough was given a special mention for her efforts in organizing the exhibition.[8] A review in the *North China Herald* singled out one of her loans: 'Mrs. Ayscough contributes among other pieces an extraordinary carved ivory figure of the god of old age standing about seven inches in height.'[9]

Ayscough's collection has been dispersed and many items have been lost, making it impossible now to judge its quality. But how did she so rapidly attain such a reputation? Bahr says that all the artworks loaned by foreigners were obtained in China 'mostly with the advice and assistance of the best native experts'. Apart from drawing on the expertise of her fellow committee members, Ayscough may have begun learning from the Latvian collector E. A. Strehlneek, who had been in China since the early 1890s. During that time he had been studying Chinese painting, and had begun to build what was then considered a formidable collection of classical masterpieces, as well as jades, ceramics, and bronzes. He assumed a Chinese name Shih Te-ni, and opened a gallery in 1910 that became a popular destination not just for Shanghai collectors but also for international visitors who occasionally mention it in letters and books. By 1913, for reasons as yet unclear, he put a substantial collection up for sale through public exhibition—a relatively modern form of art marketing that has been attributed to Japanese influence in the city. By this time Ayscough had become sufficiently well known to Strehlneek to be selected to compile the text of a handsome catalogue, entitled *Chinese Pictorial Art*, to accompany the sale. The exhibition was curtailed when the works were purchased by a Stockholm collector, Klas Fahraens, and transported to Sweden. Fahraens' intention after his death was that the pieces should be given to the Stockholm government for the people of Sweden; ultimately, however, the works were dispersed at auction, so the collection can no longer be assessed as a whole, and some items are untraced.

By this stage Ayscough wasn't yet a historian of Chinese art; the text makes clear that Strehlneek and Ayscough as 'compiler' drew heavily on Chinese sources and scholars, as well as on European texts. Although Western understanding of Chinese painting was still in its infancy, there was a realization that many paintings attributed to Tang and pre-Tang artists were in fact later copies. Still, some early attributions have not withstood later scrutiny. Despite this, Strehlneek's collection was still an influential one, not least in its role of fostering an appreciation of Chinese art among Western collectors. Handling this artwork, talking with Strehlneek, and discussing Chinese scholarship must have been truly inspirational for Ayscough. One painting accorded much space in the book and in newspapers was a snowscape attributed to the Tang-dynasty painter-poet Wang Wei. Almost certainly a copy, it would still have been an impressive artwork in its own right. Even in reproduction it has the gravitas of a minimalist masterpiece in shades of grey. To handle a work like this in the presence of a connoisseur such as Strehlneek, must have been a formative experience. Much later when Ayscough was producing her elegantly terse poetry translations, maybe the ethos of this snowscape guided her in memory.

The project would also have shown how this modern books may be beautifully crafted artifacts. *Chinese Pictorial Art* was published by the Commercial Press, its boards covered in blue brocaded silk, with gilding. In the preface Strehlneek pays tribute to the painstaking efforts of the solely Chinese management, and the high quality of the lithographic reproductions of the artworks.

Ayscough learned well. Each of her own books was to be an artifact in its own right, several of them handsomely artist-illustrated.

During the first two decades of the twentieth century, Ayscough was building a Chinese art collection that was greatly admired by Shanghai colleagues and friends. The *North China Herald* reported a visit to her collections by the American Women's Club, whose members were shown Ming-dynasty lacquer cabinets, Ming celadon, a *sang de boeuf* glazed vase, paintings, jades and stone carvings.[10] It is highly probable that she bought some of her treasures from Strehlneek, who made special efforts to market his collections to Shanghai's Western residents. For instance he welcomed a party from the American Women's Club to his home, one floor of which harked back to the Tang dynasty in its decor with padded straw matting, sliding doors with paper panes, and cabinets holding jades.[11]

A pair of *gang*, or large glazed jars, owned by Ayscough had a reputed imperial provenance. In October 1905 Ayscough had been a guest at a garden party held in the Summer Palace in Beijing. In the last years of her life the Empress Dowager Cixi received parties of foreign guests 'in an effort to placate the outer barbarians, whom she had tried in 1900 to "sweep into the sea".[12] In *Firecracker Land*, Ayscough recounted the anxiety under which they passed the summer of 1900, knowing that the Legations in Beijing were under siege by Boxer rebels, that Chinese Christians had been slaughtered, and that the Dowager Empress had called for the extermination of foreigners. One fraught night Edith Wheelock wakened the household as she had seen cannons pulled in front of their home; Francis investigated, returning with a report that a neighboring lumberyard was receiving a delivery of logs.

Five years on Florence held no expectation that an audience with the 'Old Buddha' would be anything but a necessary courtesy.

The invitation may have been arranged by Sarah Pike Conger, the wife of the American ambassador who had headed the American Legation during the Boxer Rebellion, though the Congers had left Beijing a few months previously. In Conger's correspondence to her family, later published as a bestseller entitled *Letters From China*, she wrote with surprising warmth of this woman perceived as virulently opposed to foreign presence in China, but who now graciously received parties of diplomats' wives and guests such as Ayscough, and lavished upon them hospitality, food and gifts. In an essay in *A Chinese Mirror*, Ayscough reminisced about how irreverently blasé she had been at the prospect of this audience with Cixi, which for many women represented the apogee of expatriate social success, an invitation to the ultimate A-list party. Inconveniently summoned for early morning, according to Cixi's preference, the party was obliged to set off for the Summer Palace before dawn. Ayscough had of course heard reports of Cixi's charisma, but determined not to be blinded herself by the aura of Manchu celebrity: 'My idea was that she was probably much like other old ladies.' The party was ushered into a reception room that glittered kaleidoscopically with colour and light. She was dazzled by a surge of yellow. At the core, a 'mobile face and all-seeing eyes', disturbing, irresistible. Against all intellectual and emotional objections, she was beguiled. Beside this vitality Cixi's unfortunate nephew the Guangxu Emperor seemed hunched, diminished.

A hybrid and potentially disastrous protocol: each guest mounted a flight of stairs to the throne, shook hands with the Empress who acknowledged them with a cordial 'How d'u do', shook hands with the Emperor then descended backwards—typically in high Edwardian dress, with full skirts gathered in treacherously long pleats at the back, and heeled shoes. Ayscough was uncharacteristically nauseous at the prospect of a tumble.

They managed however to retain their balance and dignity, and with relief were served lunch in a delicate pavilion, released from the presence of the Dowager Empress and Emperor. Much had been written of imperial refreshments—the multitude of tiny plates with delicate morsels. Ayscough, who was said by her family and friends to care little for ostentatious dining, remarked simply that both Chinese and European dishes were served and that they were 'delicious'. While she found the event impressive, it was hardly enjoyable. Cixi had been a gracious host, 'but it was not difficult to imagine that she was perfectly capable of exclaiming "Off with her head" as the Queen of Hearts did to Alice, and I very much doubt whether anyone present would have had the courage to reply "Nonsense".

It may have been during this visit that Ayscough was given the pair of *gang*, and an ivory comb noted by the *North China Herald* as part of her collection. The Empress Dowager had become much given to such acts of generosity, and the splendour of her beneficence had become part of Cixi-lore; Conger and her friends were the recipients of numerous gifts of expensive jewellery and decorative arts.

There was nothing unusual about Ayscough's activities as a collector. The period was one of avid accumulation of China's historic art treasures. Throughout the second and third decades of the twentieth century the *North China Herald* made numerous references to collections of artworks held privately in Shanghai, exhibitions and sales of art and antiques. Given Shanghai's recent history as a refuge for wealthy merchants and scholars from the traditional southern centres of culture, and given the wealth accumulated by foreign captains of commerce, it is little surprise that Shanghai became a treasure house. To the chagrin of cultured Chinese and long-term foreign residents, it was also a treasure house that was routinely raided when expatriates returned home with China's artistic heritage. There were repeated appeals for an art museum to be created in Shanghai (the Royal Asiatic Society maintained a museum, but it was dedicated to natural history). It was optimistically proposed that foreign residents would generously donate their collections for the benefit of the city, and in the altruistic interests of keeping Chinese art in China. During the Concession-era such an institution never materialized.

And there was nothing unusual in Ayscough's willingness to share her collections, allowing others to admire and enjoy them. It had become the mark of a connoisseur in Shanghai at least semi-publicly to display art collections. The Royal Asiatic Society supported this arrangement, often bringing together Chinese and Western collectors in pursuit of a common pleasure. One of its most popular activities was the production of several public art exhibitions each year. Ayscough was also carefully building up the library's holdings of art books, which were in heavy use.

In 1911 (as the Qing dynasty was swept away and the First Republic inaugurated) Ayscough again served with Ferguson on the organizing committee for an exhibition of Chinese paintings and bronzes. The exhibition was to be held in Sheng Xuanhuai's new library on Bubbling Well Road.[13] The august Sheng Xuanhuai (1844–1916) had been a high-ranking Qing government official, and one of Shanghai's wealthiest residents. He was a major shareholder in the China Merchants' Steam Navigation Company, of which he served as Director General. A shrewd politician, he played an active role in the Self-Strengthening Movement, and was a forceful advocate for the end of extraterritoriality (extrality). By 1911 he was President of the Board of Communications and a stalwart supporter of government-sponsored railway development. The Society's relationship with Sheng probably came about through Ferguson. Understanding education to be the route for China's development as a modern nation, Sheng in 1896 founded Nanyang College (now Shanghai Jiaotong University), where Ferguson served as the first President. Sheng and Ferguson worked very closely together until 1912.[14]

Both shared a passion for collecting books and art, and for making these accessible not just to connoisseurs, but to a wider public. Sheng intended that the imposing building on Bubbling Well Road should be open eventually as a public library. It was this space that the Royal Asiatic Society had secured for its upcoming art exhibition. The venue choice is an interesting one. The Society had successfully held art exhibitions in its own museum (it was a popular destination and in 1911 was attracting 500 Chinese visitors a day, as well as foreigners). Or it could, as it had in the past, have secured any one of the Settlement's public spaces. In the event, Sheng Xuanhuai ignominiously lost his position after violent opposition to his push for the nationalization of railways in Sichuan.[15] In the wider sphere, the overthrow of the Qing government in 1911 derailed this exhibition, and many other Society events. The planned Royal Asiatic Society alliance with Sheng Xuanhuai—reformer, educator, and advocate for a strong and independent China—might have revealed much, though, about the sympathies of Ferguson and Ayscough.

Ayscough was moving from being a connoisseur to being a curator, with all that term's modern implications not just of selection, but also of public education. In part this must have occurred from personal inclination, but a disquieting sequence of events turned proclivity into necessity. Among the Chinese scholars she counted as her friends was Liu Songfu, an elderly comprador with her husband's firm Scott, Harding and Co. Many compradors were able to take advantage of their positions straddling the Chinese and

Western worlds to develop profitable side businesses of their own. Liu was not unusual among treaty-port compradors in becoming a collector of Chinese art, as well as potentially, a dealer.[16] Long after the episode that was to cause Ayscough such anguish, she concluded, with generosity, that Liu was far more an 'old world' scholar than an astute merchant, dressing in 'an old gold robe and a short coat of crimson brocade', collecting books and paintings, and declaring the Chinese aesthete's centuries-old desire for a bucolic retirement after active service.[17] On one occasion he brought his mother to tea; she swayed on bound three-inch 'golden lilies' across the Ayscoughs' famous garden, commenting knowledge-ably on each bloom. Ayscough clearly positioned him as a gentle-man, and considered him one of her treasured teachers. In 1912 the Royal Asiatic Society organized a temporary exhibition of his modern paintings—an event that seems to have been a catalyst for his collection being chosen for exhibit at the 1915 Panama–Pacific International Exposition in San Francisco. Ayscough was commis-sioned to write a substantial catalogue—because of her obvious connection to Liu, but she had also proved herself capable of pro-ducing accessible writing on Chinese art. Her role at this seminal event was no sinecure resulting from her position as the wife of Liu's employer; more credible was her perceived ability to interest an American fair-going public in Chinese painting.

By this date China had participated in several world's fairs and major exhibitions, and understood the strategic importance of positioning itself to encourage trade and enhance diplomatic relations; however, until now the shape of this representation had been charged to the Chinese Maritime Customs Service. The Panama–Pacific Exposition was the first occasion on which the Chinese selected the exhibits and created the installations, assuming responsibility for the image of the young Republic at an event whose aim was, according to President Woodrow Wilson, 'to unite East and West'.[18]

The Chinese Ministry of Agriculture and Commerce charged major Chinese cities (including, of course, Shanghai) with identifying participants. The Shanghai Chamber of Commerce was specifically engaged to secure appropriate representation.[19] The reasons behind their selection of Liu Songfu's collection are still unclear. They may rest on the fact that these paintings had already passed the litmus test of foreign approval through the Royal Asiatic Society show.[20] Liu himself was an eager participant, as it appears he wished to sell at least part of the collection, and had already tested the waters in Shanghai. One major player in the field of Asian arts collection, though, was less content with the choice of these paintings to represent the acme of Chinese art: Detroit industrialist-turned-art-collector Charles Lang Freer (1856–1919). Freer began collecting American and European prints during the 1880s; from the end of that decade he became a passionate collector of Japanese art, only turning his full energies to acquiring Chinese art from 1909 onwards, when he made his first extended trip to China. His interests lay, almost exclusively, in pre-fourteenth century painting, and he was, in the words of one Freer scholar, 'the first American to make Chinese painting a collecting priority'.[21] By 1915 Freer had built an outstanding Chinese art collection, assisted by Asian art scholars and Chinese dealers. Freer was a member of the Panama–Pacific International Exposition's advisory committee, but as selection had been entrusted to Chinese committees, he could play no curating role in the exhibition of Chinese arts.

He had known about Liu's collection for several years, and had asked an unnamed Chinese expert to examine it in Shanghai. The expert's cabled response was that it contained 'nothing of real importance' to the collector. Freer then visited the works on display in San Francisco in 1915, and expressed his displeasure to the Exposition's Director of Fine Arts, John Trask: 'I saw enough to convince me that they represented ancient Chinese painting most unworthily.'[22] Freer believed the American public should have been exposed to what he believed to be much more eminent collections. In retrospect, maybe it wasn't eminence but reassurance that was the then perceived strength of Liu's collection.[23] The bulk of the works were pre-Modern, and were at the time attributed to Ming and pre-Ming artists. They were, for the most part, landscapes and historical subjects of the type that American audiences were beginning to appreciate, or at least become familiar with.

Ayscough's catalogue was meticulously compiled, and followed the attributions of the most respected Chinese experts of the period. She wasn't attempting to contribute original scholarship, but instead illuminate the subject for an interested general public. Accepting that her readership was not the scholarly audience of the Royal Asiatic Society back in Shanghai, she gave much of her text over to explanations of subject matter that would have been foreign to Californian eyes. She provides biographical information on artists whose names might have been unpronounceable, and draws attention to realistic details such as the quivering eyes of peacocks' tails—perhaps in an effort to compensate for a lack of the Western perspective or tonal modelling more familiar to a Western audience. The Chinese delegation was received with the requisite ceremony, China had its 'day' during the nine-and-a-half-month run of the exposition, yet the anticipated sales were disappointing. Two years later one of Ayscough's friends recalled, 'The great American public, as you know, has little understanding of Chinese painting and though these were well placed in the Exhibition, they attracted practically no buyers. Under my advice my sister-in-law purchased several very beautiful pieces at prices that I considered Chinese, and not foreign.'[24]

One buyer who may have found the prices attractive was the Baltimore industrialist Henry Walters who purchased 52 catalogue items that became part of the collections of the Walters Art Museum in Baltimore.[25] In terms of quality and authenticity, this group is now considered weak—except, that is, for an album of sixteen paintings by artists who had been active in Shanghai in the latter half of the twentieth century.[26] One example from this album is an ink painting on paper, *Playing the Flute*, by one of the best known of this group, the Shanghai Modernist Ren Bonian (1840–95) (*Plate 1*). Other larger works by Ren Bonian went unsold at this time and it is not difficult to see why such a work might have been puzzling to an American audience. The favourably reviewed paintings on exhibit at the fair included the assured society portraiture of John Singer Sargent, and the soft, bucolic landscapes of American Impressionists such as Childe Hassam. By contrast Ren Bonian's work belongs to another world. It employs blank white paper to stand in for solid surfaces, a facility Ayscough described as 'an extraordinary sense of the value of empty space'.[27] Looming in the left foreground is an unmodelled blue mass. Other areas such as the gnarled bark of the trees are almost frantically detailed. Compared with, say, Sargent's completely graspable portrait of the novelist Henry James, the Ren Bonian would have seemed eccentric to most viewers.

Ayscough considered such Qing-dynasty artists interesting, talented, energetic, but inferior to their predecessors. This was a view she shared with most early Western historians of Chinese art. However, the collector Liu Songfu highly valued modern works such as these, and for years focused his collecting on the group of artists who have become known as the Shanghai School. Although the paintings on display in San Francisco in 1915 from Liu's collection were largely older works, they did include a sizable collection of modern paintings—and it was, ironically, modern paintings that participating countries were invited to display at the exposition. It is an example of the twists of taste that punctuate art history that now the works of Ren Bonian and his contemporary Xu Gu are considered among the most important of Liu Songfu's former collection. Ren Bonian is now so acceptable to American public taste that a reproduction of a painting bequeathed to the Art Institute of Chicago after Ayscough's death is, at the time of writing, for sale in the museum shop.

The preface to the catalogue is an 'address' to Liu Songfu, translated from the Chinese. One passage, though at the time possibly conventional praise, leaps out as ominously clairvoyant: 'Whenever he comes across a valuable piece, he does not stint any amount of money to acquire it. Through his sedulous efforts for several decades, he has secured several hundred pieces of great worth and beauty.'[28] For all that he held a position of considerable responsibility as the comprador of a large import house, Liu Songfu, in his richly coloured silk clothing, was, according to Ayscough, a deeply unworldly person, ill-attuned to the demands of commercial life in Shanghai. Even after the financial cataclysm he was to cause her household, Ayscough diagnosed his character as discomfited, rather than malicious: 'Those types of the old school, of which our old Comprador was one, sit in dazed bewilderment watching their "gods" crash about them—feeling that the world is travelling too fast for their comprehension.'[29]

Soon after the Panama–Pacific exhibit Liu Songfu died, leaving his accounts with Scott, Harding and Co. in disarray. Badly indebted, the firm took possession of his collection as compensation and Florence was charged with the burden of finding buyers.

Disheartened by memories of the sluggish market for Chinese art in 1915, she wrote to her childhood friend Amy Lowell, who instantly cabled to invite her to Sevenels to devise a plan of action. Lowell was a bulwark. Ayscough recalled, 'It is quite impossible for me to express what an *immense* difference that cable made to me. The matter in hand was certainly difficult, and my heart sank low at the prospect before me...'[30] A travel-worn and anxious Ayscough arrived on a deserted railway platform in Boston on a dark November night in 1917. The chill and grime of the station were instantly dispelled by the warmth and ebullience of the friend who came to meet her.

Ayscough's first course of action was to contact the most respected authority on Asian art in North America: Charles Lang Freer. In her correspondence she revealed no knowledge of Freer's earlier antipathy to Liu's collection, approaching him instead through the connection with the North China Branch of the Royal Asiatic Society. John Ferguson was one of Freer's advisors; in the Smithsonian Freer Gallery of Art is a magnificent Southern Song-dynasty ink-on-silk hand scroll, *Nymph of the Luo River*, attributed to Gu Kaizhi, whose provenance is Duanfang's collection, via Ferguson.[31] Probably through Ferguson's influence Freer made several donations to the Royal Asiatic Society library in Shanghai. Earlier in 1917 he had given a photographic reproduction of a scroll then attributed to the Song-dynasty painter Ma Yuan.[32]

Hearing that Freer had fallen ill, Ayscough delayed a few days before writing to him on 12 December:

> I wonder if you will remember my name? As Hon. Librarian North China Branch of the Royal Asiatic Soc. mine has been the pleasant task of acknowledging various gifts of yours to the Society. I am now in America in connection with the sale of a collection

of Chinese painting—my first thought upon arrival a few days ago was to write to you ... I will not worry you with the details of how the paintings came into my possession—it is a long and tragic tale—but I write to ask advice of you as the person best qualified to give it as to the best method of disposing of Chinese painting. In the collection there are pictures of great beauty and interest of various periods ... Please pardon my worrying of you—for all who are lovers of the Far East know that you are the one person who would do everything possible to make the Great World of the Orient comprehensible to the busy West.[33]

Ayscough could hardly have chosen a less propitious introduction. If Freer did recognize her name her letter may well have triggered unhappy memories of another discomfiting incident involving Liu Songfu's collection. Ayscough refrains from mentioning Liu by name, but it is quite probable Freer made the connection. In November 1914 Freer had been introduced to a young Chinese art agent, Lee Kee Son, claiming to be from a formerly wealthy family now in impoverished exile because of their political allegiances. Freer, in fact, knew Lee's father, the wealthy Shanghai merchant and collector Li Ping-shu from previous collecting trips to Shanghai.[34] Lee explained that because of the former prominence of his family, he had access to rare paintings which he begged Freer to buy, or help him sell, to support his family. Over the following months Lee sent Freer batches of paintings, few of which interested the eminent collector, though he bought some for relatively minor sums of money. On 31 August 1915, Lee shipped Freer three cases containing 87 paintings 'property Liu Sung Fu', for which Freer paid him US$5,250. Freer's intention seems to have been to sell these works. Three weeks later events took a most disquieting turn when Freer was informed that Lee had absconded with his money leaving Liu without payment or paintings. Within a few days Lee was arrested in Berkeley, CA. He was contrite. He claimed the whole affair had been a misunderstanding. To the Berkeley police he stated that he had mortgaged Liu's paintings to assist his family now in Kobe, Japan; in a letter of 6 October to Freer he explained his motives rather differently: 'The Young China party in which I am interested is in financial difficulty, so I only meant to place Mr. Liu's painting in your custody in order to get some cash money as a sort of advancement to further the revolutionary movement.'[35]

Neither Liu nor Freer seems to have pressed charges, the paintings were returned to Liu, and Freer retrieved his money. But the matter was certainly a messy and time-consuming affair for Freer; he had begun to disperse the paintings and had to scramble to stop a sale. So Ayscough's letter two years later, at a time when he was debilitated by illness, can hardly have been welcome. His response the next day was disappointing:

> During the last four or five years many small and large lots of Chinese paintings have been brought to America and offered through various channels to an uneducated public. Quite a number of the specimens brought were disposed of at varying figures, some of which were ridiculously high and others absurdly low.
>
> Because of the lack of expert opinion, such of the buyers as purchased the poorer objects became discouraged and are not likely to buy any more Chinese pictures until they have achieved greater knowledge themselves or shall have found some competent person willing to advise them. Other more fortunate purchasers who by accident happened to secure important specimens view the situation differently and are as a rule ready to take their chances, but the majority of this class recognize the desirability of

expert advice and are less ready than before to buy things brought to them from any direction, even the few dealers of experience.

Freer regretted that his illness and prior demands on his time prevented him from viewing in person Ayscough's collection, concluding with words that may have been slighting, but also contained the seed for her future actions:

> As you know, I am deeply interested in helping to make known in America the best Oriental ancient art, and I am equally opposed to inferior specimens finding anchorage in the United States. I have already helped to send back to China much trash that was offered or about to be offered to American buyers, and on the other hand have aided to a considerable extent every effort that has come to my attention to place in American public and private collections such objects of ancient Chinese art as I believed to be valuable as objects of real aesthetic value.[36]

If the key to enlightened collecting was better education, then Ayscough would pursue every path to bring to the collecting public opportunities to learn more about Chinese art. From today's perspective, the curatorial activities she undertook—at short notice and in the short span of time until spring 1918—were prodigious. Spurred by necessity, this self-described 'retiring' person embarked on a campaign to vigorously market this collection via the avenues of the New York art market and major American art institutions. If she perceived Freer's letter as a rebuff, she did not allow it to dent her confidence in the quality of the art she was attempting to disperse.

By mid-February she was able to tell Lowell that she had lectured twice in New York, and was about to open a ten-day exhibition at Gertrude Vanderbilt Whitney's Studio, which hosted groundbreaking exhibitions of modern art. She was also negotiating an exhibit at Knoedler and Company's gallery. She had rented an apartment in Manhattan for private viewings, and in February and March she lectured at the Colony Club and the Cosmopolitan Club, both prestigious women's institutions.[37] In April she exhibited at the Rhode Island School of Design, and lectured on Chinese mortuary art—objects placed in tombs to accompany and protect the dead. According to an account pasted into a scrapbook of clippings in the Rhode Island School of Design archives she was an entertaining lecturer, authoritative, but with a keen sense of how to capture her audience's imaginations. These artworks were part of a 'world of shades' where the living were entombed with the dead to comfort and entertain them. Slowly, she managed to sell a small part of the collection.

Increasingly she was realizing that her collection of modern paintings was of special value, as these seemed to point a way forward for a tradition that some regarded moribund:

> The pictures painted by men who died just before the fateful year 1900 are especially interesting in that, although untouched by any influence of Western technique, they reveal the restless spirit which prevailed at the end of the century, and to all who look forward to the Renaissance their freshness and virility must bring hope of things that are to be.[38]

A 1917 photograph, which was probably taken as a publicity shot, shows Ayscough in New York, in a loose 'oriental' robe posed in front of Ren Bonian's *The Five Relationships* (1895) (*Figure 6*). She is elegant, handsomely strong-featured, and wearing the opals without which she felt 'not fully dressed'. She had begun to understand that lecturing was performance, requiring poise and

Figure 6 Florence Ayscough in New York, 1917. Photograph reproduced in *The Incomparable Lady*.

presence, and a keen sense of pitch. In February of that year she had delivered a lecture to the Royal Asiatic Society in Shanghai to standing room only.[39] She was adopting the dramatic sense of dress that would be regularly noted in newspapers, and building a reputation of her own. Doubtless she was encouraged in this by Lowell, who in turn had been coached by her actress partner Russell to make poetry readings events of great drama and spectacle. Lowell ranged between shouts, whispers, foot-stamping, and long moments of suspenseful silence. If, like Lowell, Ayscough had infamously smoked cigars before and after performances the press would surely have seized on it. Less flamboyantly, she had learnt to manipulate tone and tempo, and to include impactful visual aids in the form of her own art collections and slides from her photographs.

Ren Bonian's *The Five Relationships* must have been a favourite; it would continue to have deep meaning for her throughout her life, and much later it inspired the name of her home in Chicago. In her exhibition catalogue she wrote that it was the best of the artist's bird studies, with the birds symbolizing the Chinese concept of the cardinal human relationships ranging from sovereign and subject, to father and son, brothers, husband and wife and friends. In concept and execution, it suggested perfection.

At the Whitney Studio galleries these modern paintings were particularly admired by artists who dubbed them 'the oriental impressionists'. Knowing that the general public's taste would be challenged by these, she was making a special effort to place her modern works with museums, hoping for a more enlightened reception. Through a friend she contacted Frederic Whiting, Director of the Cleveland Museum of Art, explaining, 'I know that the very words "modern Chinese" are anathema! Nevertheless these pictures will I think arouse great interest, they are very full of life, very virile, impressionistic, yet thoroughly characteristic of the East.'[40] Whiting did not want to acquire any for the museum, but he did arrange a beautifully presented exhibition at the museum (*Figure 7*) and a travelling exhibition that toured to major Midwestern art museums, including the Art Institute of Chicago. The tour continued until the spring of 1920, when it was cancelled because of damage to some of the paintings.

Ayscough hoped that after the Great War a museum would purchase the collection as a whole. This didn't happen, but after

Figure 7 Gallery View Photographs, Gallery 10, Chinese Paintings and Calligraphy lent by Mrs. Florence Ayscough, 6 July–6 August 1919. The Cleveland Museum of Art Archives, Records of the Registrar's Office. Photograph © The Cleveland Museum of Art.

her death most of these works were bequeathed to the Art Institute of Chicago, and have become a prized aspect of their Chinese collections, exhibited most recently as a group in 2006. Despite the short-term failure of her efforts to find a buyer, she deserves credit for promoting the appreciation of early Chinese Modernism in America.

In 1917 selling the art collection was her main objective, but it was the strategy she employed—enlightening the public about the paintings and their cultural background—that provided the kernel for the next breakthrough in her career as a writer. Just as the bleakness of that late night Boston railway platform back in November 1917 was transformed by Amy Lowell's presence, so was her task of decoding the script on the calligraphic scrolls she hoped to explain through her public lectures.

3
Words
The 'sensuous realist'[1]

In the twenty years since Ayscough and Lowell had been young women together in Boston, Lowell had been forging her own successful path as a poet and by 1917 had published three poetry collections. One of these, *Sword Blades and Poppy Seed* (1914) had been a critically acclaimed bestseller that catapulted Lowell into celebrity, while her public persona became a lure for controversy. Openly lesbian, obese, cigar-smoking and bellicose, she had become infamous for her feud with the Modernist poet Ezra Pound over 'ownership' of the poetic avant-garde. The details of this wrangle reflect on the project she was about to embark upon with Ayscough. In 1913, while Ayscough was delving into Chinese painting, Lowell discovered Imagism. A loosely-connected group of British and American poets, now recognized as incipient Modernists, the Imagists rejected traditional poetic conventions and adopted free verse, aspiring to reflect the cadences of everyday speech. Drawing on her ample financial resources and her influential social and publishing networks, Lowell was able to champion and promote this new group of writers, who included Hilda Doolittle (who wrote simply as 'H. D.'), Ford Madox Ford, and Richard Aldington. Her initial friendship with Pound soured, and he refused to participate in the anthologies of Imagist poets that Lowell edited in 1915, 1916 and 1917.

When Ayscough turned to Lowell for help at the end of 1917, she was requesting not just the consolations of friendship but also Lowell's assistance as an established poet. If Ayscough was to sell her collection of Chinese paintings and calligraphy in America, she needed to make them as accessible as possible; obviously, her calligraphic paintings required compelling translations. She brought some rough attempts to Lowell, hoping her friend could transform them into something more poetic. Lowell was immediately captivated, explaining, 'I was fascinated by the poems, and, as we talked them over, we realized that here was a field in which we would like to work.'[2] What started as a favour turned into a four-year collaboration resulting in the 1921 publication of *Fir-Flower Tablets*. This book would contain some startlingly beautiful translations of poets already familiar to the West, and would also introduce some previously untranslated poetry.

Their work together was a four-year 'paper hunt' across continents and oceans. Lowell knew no Chinese; Ayscough wasn't a poet. But working together they believed they were producing work in translation superior to anything published by their contemporaries. Having translated enough of the scrolls for Ayscough to use in her lectures, they decided to embark upon the enterprise of translating several of China's most revered classical poets, including Li Po, Tu Fu and Wang Wei. In doing so they entered into territory fiercely contested by some of the West's most eminent sinologists and poets. Inevitably there were skirmishes and casualties, but their work was to both women 'a continually augmenting pleasure'.[3]

The process, though, was an arduous one. Ayscough would write out each poem word by word for Lowell, giving several meanings for each character. Sometimes she provided an explanation of the characters' etymology. She also provided diligent and copious notes to help Lowell understand the historical and geographical context and the literary allusions. Lowell then used this as the raw material for creating poetry 'as near the originals as we could make them', while still being satisfying creations in the English language. When they were together they worked until 2 a.m. Lowell, whose energies were legendary and output prodigious, would continue to work alone through the night, leaving little yellow slips with notes for Ayscough to retrieve the next morning. When Ayscough was in St. Andrews the telephone would habitually ring at midnight, and Florence would rouse herself from bed to perch in her nightgown, responding down a crackling line as to whether the words were *tui tzu* or *toi tao*. They frequently agreed to disagree; after such a long friendship Ayscough must have learned her own way of deflecting Lowell's 'scorpion' words, spoken in a flash of anger, though arguing with Lowell 'was like plunging into a deep blue wave'.[4] When she returned to China the process was complicated further by war-delayed mail. Lowell would send the manuscripts back to Ayscough via the *Empress of Asia*, or another of the liners that plied the Pacific, to be pored over by Ayscough and her teacher Nung Chu—the last and most inspiring of a series of teachers she worked with in Shanghai. Some of the poems made the return trip across the Pacific to Vancouver, then by rail to New England, several times.

By the start of this project Ayscough was already deeply immersed in the study of Chinese language and culture; *Fir-Flower Tablets* was a natural outcome of her interests. What motivated Lowell (beyond loyalty to a friend) was her immediate identification with the Chinese work Ayscough brought her. Lowell found in Chinese poetry values similar to those she espoused for herself and the Imagists. The preface to her 1915 anthology outlines the movement's precepts:

> To present an image (hence the name: 'Imagist'). We are not a school of painters, but we believe that poetry should render particulars exactly and not deal in vague generalities, however magnificent and sonorous … To produce poetry that is hard and clear, never blurred nor indefinite. Finally, most of us believe that concentration is of the very essence of poetry.[5]

A Lowell poem in this anthology and a *Fir-Flower Tablets* translation are markedly similar:

> Grass-blades push up between the cobblestones
> And catch the sun on their flat sides
> Shooting it back,
> Gold and emerald,
> Into the eyes of passers-by.
>
> Lowell, from The Travelling Bear

> Again the white water flower
> Is ripe for plucking.
> The green, pointed swords of the iris
> Splinter the brown earth.[6]
>
> Liu Shih-An (calligrapher),
from One Goes a Journey in Fir-Flower Tablets

There is the same intense concentration on a visual image, the same economy of words, the same insistence on a few well-chosen verbs rather than a pile-up of adjectives. There is nothing 'blurred or indefinite' in the splintering of soil. Of course, the Chinese poem is, rather, 'Ayscough and Lowell'. 'Splinter' is their word. But another time and culture's poetry is seen through the lens of our own, just as translation is rooted in its own time and place. It was as an Imagist poet that Lowell approached Chinese poetry, and as an early twentieth-century critic that Ayscough could write of poems written in calligraphy: 'A beautiful thought perpetuated in beautiful handwriting and hung upon the wall to suggest a mental picture—does not the possession of such a medium rouse the envy of Occidental imagists, who are indeed the spiritual descendants of the East?'[7]

The dedication to choosing the *exact* words, shaped by Lowell's Imagism and Ayscough's diligence, attracted a minor squall of criticism that marred the reception of *Fir-Flower Tablets*. In attempting to 'burrow' out the allusions of characters, Ayscough at times delved into their etymology, justifying this by reasoning that for an educated Chinese reader, a character's etymology would always be present in his mind. This was not a major feature of the translations, though, as Lowell explains, 'The analysis of characters has been employed very rarely, and only when the text seemed to lean on the allusion for an added vividness or zest.'[8] That critics should have seized negatively on this is a pity, as the device was seldom employed. A much more salient feature of the poetry was the authors' concern with accuracy and explanation.

In her own introduction Ayscough explains the difficulty she is trying to resolve when she asks the reader to imagine how a Chinese poet in a grass hut would understand Amy Lowell's poem *Nostalgia* without an intermediary. *Nostalgia* offers a brief sequence of images, but for a Western reader it conveys a world of allusion to rail travel, marble-floored hotels with bellboys and elevators—allusions utterly inaccessible to the Chinese poet. Ayscough's point is that the Chinese world is just as alien to Westerners without a guide. To orient her readers to this world, Ayscough wrote a lengthy introduction describing China's topography, climate, and political and social history. This was appreciated by *The New York*

Times reviewer as providing 'a more illuminating notion of China generally than any number of dry-as-dust treatises'.[9]

Fir-Flower Tablets is a collection of poetry, but it is also a guide to China's culture and natural history. And it was Ayscough's direct experience of nature in China, her childhood of horses and gardens and riverboats, and her observational acuity, that brought such diversity of natural species, nuance of colour and textural depth to those translations. In terms of flora and fauna, *Fir-Flower Tablets* is a species-rich celebration of the natural world. In a letter to the *China Journal of Science and Arts* (the publication of the Shanghai Museum and long edited by the Museum's curator and a Society president for a time, Arthur de Carle Sowerby) Ayscough notes their ornithological precision:

> I find that in our collection of one hundred and thirty-seven pieces, among the birds referred to are: kites, vultures, nightingales, yellow geese, wild geese, magpies, orioles, swallows, parrots, white herons, yellow herons, mandarin ducks, jackdaws, gulls, pheasants, cocks and chickens, to say nothing of the fabulous birds such as the Silver-crested Love Pheasant, the Green Fire-bird, and the Jade Love-bird.[10]

By contrast, it was a perceived lack of ornithological accuracy that attracted one of Ayscough's few negative public comments about Arthur Waley, the *eminence grise* of Chinese translation. His mistranslation of a line suggesting that the poet *saw* (rather than heard) the reclusive golden oriole was, according to Ayscough, '… a mistake which every naturalist would condemn'. While she acknowledged that although Waley—who had never been, and would never go, to China—could produce 'exquisite' poetry, he lacked 'a certain vividness of perception, a vividness which only a visual experience of

China could give him.'[11] Years later, in a letter to her close friend Mary Matteson Wilber, she described a distinct *modus operandi* amongst the art historians of Europe whose comprehension of China was 'purely academic', and who studied Chinese art 'as if it were the art of Egypt say, of a people who have entirely departed from the realm of actuality …'[12] Whether writing on art, or translating poetry, Ayscough believed that the decades she lived in China contributed so many more dimensions to her work.

At their most satisfying, the *Fir-Flower* translations are pared to their pith:

> Shoals of fish assemble and scatter,
> Suddenly there is no trace of them.
>
> The single butterfly comes—
> Goes—
> Comes—
> Returning as though urged by love.[13]
>
> Ho Shao-Chi (calligrapher)

Sometimes, they seem burdened by particulars, and the demands of compass precision. While some lines are sharp and fresh, others feel overworked, exhausted perhaps by their transpacific excursions. This can be sensed by comparing the opening lines of the Ayscough/Lowell translation of Li Po's *Saying Good-Bye to a Friend* with a much looser one by Ezra Pound, who relied almost entirely on the notes of Ernest Fenollosa, an American scholar who studied Chinese poetry in Japan:

> Clear green hills at a right angle to the North wall,
> White water winding to the East of the city.
> Here is the place where we must part.
> The lonely water-plants go ten thousand *li*;[14]
>
> Ayscough/Lowell

> Blue mountains to the north of the walls,
> White river winding about them;
> Here we must make separation
> And go out through a thousand miles of dead grass.[15]
>
> Ezra Pound

Lowell was predictably acerbic about Pound's inaccuracies in his groundbreaking and much lauded *Cathay* (1915), and his cribbing of Fenollosa's translations. The literary critic in her nevertheless admitted that although 'they are not what he says they are', she couldn't deny they were beautiful.[16] Just as their own translations could be, when they leaned most on sensory experience of China:

> Every time I have started for the Yellow Flower River,
> I have gone down the Blue-Green Stream,
> Following the hills, making ten thousand turnings.
> We go along rapidly, but advance scarcely one
>   hundred *li*.
> We are in the midst of a noise of water,
> Of the confused and mingled sounds of water broken
>   by stones,
> And in the deep darkness of pine-trees.
> Rocked, rocked,
> Moving on and on,
> We float past water-chestnuts
> Into a still clearness reflecting reeds and rushes.
> My heart is clean and white as silk; it has already
>   achieved Peace;
> It is smooth as the placid river.
> I long to stay here, curled up on the rocks,
> Dropping my fish-line forever.[17]
>
> Wang Wei, *The Blue-Green Stream*

The still water reflecting rushes, the sensation of rocking, floating, and the calmness of a heart 'clean and white as silk' may well draw on echoes of childhood experience on Chinese houseboats. When Ayscough referred to another Chinese poet (Li Po) as a 'sensuous realist' she might just as well have been describing herself.

A comparison with a translation of the same poem by their contemporary, the American poet and writer Witter Bynner (Bynner visited, rather than lived in, China), underscores the sensory richness of the Ayscough/Lowell version:

> I have sailed the River of Yellow Flowers,
> Borne by the channel of a green stream,
> Rounding ten thousand turns through the mountains
> On a journey of less than thirty miles …
> Rapids hum over heaped rocks;
> But where light grows dim in the thick pines,
> The surface of an inlet sways with nut-horns
> And weeds are lush along the banks.
> … Down in my heart I have always been as pure
> As this limpid water is …
> Oh, to remain on a broad flat rock,
> And to cast a fishing-line forever![18]
>
> Wang Wei, *A Green Stream*

The Bynner version is a visual description; the Ayscough/Lowell one is a sensory experience.

Although Ayscough was usually a generous critic, quick to see the worth in others' efforts ('the last thing I want to do is "throw bricks"—it is the *curse* of sinology'[19]), Bynner stimulated an atypically hostile response from her. She and Lowell certainly considered him irreverent (he had spoofed Imagism in a 1916 publication *Spectra: A Book of Poetic Experiments*). In part it was personal; Bynner coined the cruel moniker *hippopoetess* for Lowell, which quickly gained currency in literary circles. Maybe more significantly, Ayscough recognized that their approaches to translation were completely divergent. In her eyes he was uncommitted, impressionistic rather than precise, shoddy in his workmanship. He lacked heft: 'It is very simple to work the way Bynner does: what he doesn't understand he leaves out!'[20]

Bynner was an amateur without the love. He came out to China and galloped through 300 Tang poems. A letter Ayscough wrote to him from Yokohama aboard the *Empress of Asia* crackles with frustration. Ayscough's letters are often beautiful artifacts in themselves, either typed, or written in purple ink on paper decorated with a pine needle motif, plus her personal seal. This one was written with such emotion that it jammed in the typewriter. It is blotched, full of crosses and corrections; even her irreproachable grammar deserts her. It does, though, contain the kernel of her belief about translation. She understood herself as a craftsman, who had served a long, self-abnegating apprenticeship, and who now approached her work in a spirit of veneration:

> You see, so far, with the exception of Mr. Waley's, the translation have been very very poor & have misrepresented the Chinese poets in the most appalling manner, I had hoped that we had had enough of these approximations, this 'giving of the idea'. What I feel about your work is that if the Angel Gabriel himself under-took it he could not make a scholarly pices [*sic*: piece] of work. Therefore it must be another approximation. What I know of it bristles with inaccuracies. It is not your fault, it is that you are trying to do an impossible thing. Of course it may bring you a certain amount of 'kudos'—but it—is very hard on the T'ang poets....
>
> Although it is not possible to render the delicacy, the subtlety, the beauty of Chinese poetry, in its marvellous terseness, if one works reverently, & humbly, if one studies without cease, if one spares no time

or strength (a short poem often takes three days of hard work) one must surely produce something that is faithful to the spirit of these great men—& that is what working on the lines you are doing it is not possible to accomplish. Of course I do not suppose that you can care as I do—but there it is.[21]

Knowledge is pleasure—and also passion.

Plate 1 Ren Bonian, *Playing the Flute*, ink and colour on paper mounted on cloth. Acquired by Henry Walters, 1915. The Walters Art Museum.

Plate 2 Eva Dunlap, watercolour of 72 Penang Road, 1935. By permission of Dorothea Mordan.

Plate 3 China, *Hanging*, Ming dynasty (1368–1644), 1601/50, Silk and gold-leaf-over-lacquered-paper-strip-wrapped silk, slit tapestry weave with interlaced outlining wefts; painted details, 236.5 x 171.3cm, Florence Ayscough and Harley Farnsworth MacNair Collection, 1943.17, The Art Institute of Chicago.

Plate 4 Wax-resist cotton bib, collection Logan Museum of Anthropology, Beloit College.

Plate 5 Topside, St. Andrews, New Brunswick (now the Kingsbrae Arms). By permission of Harry Chancey.

Plate 6 Memorial window in St. James the Great, Cradley, Herefordshire, dedicated by Florence Ayscough. By permission of Andrew Loutit.

4

Gardens and the Grass Hut

'A liberal education'[1]

On 11 February 1922 Florence Ayscough wrote to tell Amy Lowell that she and Francis had come to 'a very momentous decision, which is this. Frank will retire from the firm at the end of this year. We shall sell this house, and, sometime next spring, will come and make St. Andrews our headquarters.'[2] In 1922 Francis was 63 years old; he had been in China for over thirty years. He may already have been suffering the symptoms of the disease that would slowly and painfully debilitate him over the next decade. Most of Florence's family connections in Shanghai had already been severed. Her parents had returned to the United States in the first decade of her marriage. Settling in Boston, her father Thomas had maintained his ties with Asia, becoming first President of the East Asiatic Society of Boston, and Honorary Japanese Consul.[3] Her mother Edith died of pneumonia in 1913. Towards the end of his life Thomas lived in Shanghai with the Ayscoughs, and died in January 1920. He was buried in the Bubbling Well Cemetery. Around the same time, her younger brother Geoffrey had fallen ill with influenza, pleurisy and typhoid. Divorced from his first wife Mary, he had become engaged to his New Brunswick second cousin, Lois Grimmer, 'a fine creature', according to Florence, who hoped she would bring her brother marital happiness 'after all his misery'.[4] Geoffrey recovered enough to sail to Canada in January, and marry Grimmer on 24 February 1920 in New Brunswick. But by June he was dead of pleurisy.[5] Lois moved to Shanghai to join her sister-in-law, was quickly adopted by the 'sporting set' and Geoffrey's old friends, and was engaged by the end of the year.

Although Francis was keen to return to St. Andrews, Florence, after the publication of *Fir-Flower Tablets*, was conflicted about leaving China. The book had generally been favourably reviewed in China and the West, and had placed Ayscough and Lowell on the map as translators worthy of critical and popular attention. *The New York Times* deemed it 'a remarkable triumph', identifying Ayscough as 'richly and delicately endowed with the literary sense'—an accolade that must have bolstered her confidence as a newly published writer. Reginald Johnston, tutor to China's last emperor Puyi, had acquired a copy for his teenage charge. Now Ayscough wanted to focus on the poets Tu Fu and Wang Wei. After a succession of four language tutors, she had found in the fifth, the Nanjing scholar Nung Chu, a teacher, treasured counsellor and friend. She briefly considered bringing him with them to Canada. It may have been as a compromise to his wife that Francis agreed that they keep a Shanghai *pied-à-terre*, in which they could sometimes spend the winters. By July the foundations were laid for a modest single-storey Chinese courtyard house in a corner of the expansive gardens at 60 Gordon Road. The process of building the 'Grass Hut' was 'a liberal education' in itself, documented through her diary. This house was significant enough for Ayscough to include a detailed essay on it in *A Chinese Mirror* (1925). It was a culmination of her China years, and also a repository for her learning on Chinese culture and her art collections. The house has been gone since the late 1930s, but striking pen and ink drawings in *A*

Chinese Mirror document its appearance, and its entrance is visible in Ayscough's 1934 Christmas card. The most complete representation, though, is a delicate watercolour from 1935 by Eva Dunlap (*Plate 2*). Eva and Albert Menzo Dunlap had arrived in China in 1911, shortly after their marriage. Dr. Albert Dunlap began a long medical practice in China, while his wife pursued her art, producing thousands of paintings and drawings during the couple's long sojourn in China.[6] Dunlap became acquainted with Ayscough in 1912, and like many others, attested to the beauty of both homes on the Gordon Road site, Ayscough's hospitality and her influence and inspiration as a teacher and friend.

This home had as much outdoor as indoor space (*Figure 8*). Throughout her adult life Florence was a passionate gardener, creating exquisite grounds in Shanghai, St. Andrews, Guernsey and Chicago. She and Francis were prominent members of the Shanghai Horticultural Society—another institution that shaped Shanghailander life, but one that also fostered friendships and exchange of knowledge between foreigners and Chinese. Initially she practised Western gardening, and the grounds of 60 Gordon Road were laid out as an elegantly informal British garden, with well-tended lawns, shade trees and flower beds. But as she became immersed in Chinese theories of landscape design, she looked for an opportunity to experiment with these ideas and with native plants. The courtyard gardens she created for the Grass Hut were a radical departure from her earlier ones, and from the gardens of the vast majority of foreign settlers in Shanghai.

According to Harley MacNair, Ayscough's love of gardening was an extension of her love of the natural world: 'Florence hated to be shut in by either walls or mountains or to be cut off from immediate touch with the earth … Elemental, she loved the vastness of the sea, with its eternal movement, and wanted to work in the soil,

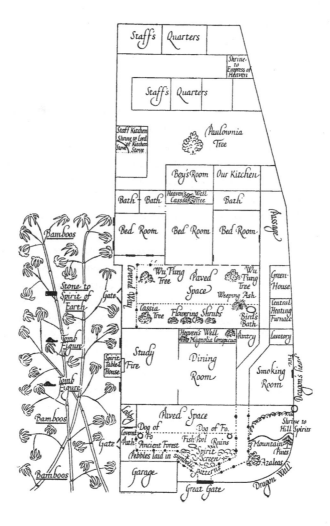

Figure 8 Floor plan and gardens, 72 Penang Road, Shanghai. From *A Chinese Mirror*. This house was built on the Ayscoughs' Gordon Road property.

to plant seeds and watch them grow, to put on old clothes, kneel on a mat, and dig weeds from flowerbeds and lawns.'[7] Ironically, Shanghai in all its clotted density gave her the opportunity to cultivate her gardening skills. Photographs of the Ayscoughs' first new house in 1903 show a scrubby, raw-looking landscape. By the time the couple sold the larger parcel of their property, its extensive grounds had become well known, and consistently produced prize-winning specimens at Horticultural Society shows.

The Shanghai Horticultural Society had been founded in 1875 with the dual aims of encouraging amateur gardeners in the beautification of what was considered an 'unlovely' city, and more scientifically, promoting horticultural knowledge. The standard of exhibits at its public flower shows (the first of which was held in the grounds of the British Consulate on 29 May 1875) became a benchmark of its progress. Francis Ayscough was a long-serving member of the committee, and a frequent judge and prizewinner. Florence too was actively involved in promoting the Society's work, and the couple's 'strenuous efforts' were credited with bolstering Society membership.[8] Both were well known enough in horticultural circles to serve later on the committee of the British Flower Shop, which opened on Kiangse Road in March 1916 as a patriotic effort to undermine the profits of the German florists who had operated so successfully in Shanghai.[9]

As a prominent Shanghailander, Francis was also a member of the Parks Committee, set up in 1906 by the Municipal Council to oversee the Settlement's parks. The previous year Donald MacGregor, a trained horticulturalist from the Royal Botanic Gardens, Kew, had been appointed by the Municipal Council as the Superintendent of Parks and Gardens. His background in Western concepts of public parks and their recreational and educational functions, plus his scientific knowledge of Chinese trees and plants, would significantly shape Shanghai's 'parkscape' over his 24-year tenure.[10] He was also a keen supporter of the Horticultural Society, and certainly influenced the Ayscoughs' approach to gardening.

The earlier gardens of 60 Gordon Road are described by Yo Fei, the little pug Florence bought as a puppy in Weihaiwei, and ventriloquized in the charmingly quirky *The Autobiography of a Chinese Dog* (1926). There were lush, rolling lawns, and an aged camphor tree under which a very proper British afternoon tea was served, complete with linen and silverware. There were tea parties and garden parties and a memorable night-time lantern dance, in which three swaying dragons glided over the lawns to gongs and drum beats, applauded by an audience of hundreds. On this occasion, outside the Ayscoughs' gates decorum collapsed into disorder. The 50 men in each dragon, from different villages, had a teahouse altercation so unruly that the district magistrate rather unfairly forbade a repeat performance.

The sylvan grounds hosted a more sedate party in June 1919, when the Ayscoughs held a private sweet pea competition, inspiring the *North China Herald* correspondent to lavish praise: 'Rustic seats and tables were temptingly placed under the refreshing shelter of outstretched trees and to sit awhile in the midst of nature's wealth of beauty was to attune visitors to a right sense of the glorious shades and colours of the wonderful collection of sweet peas …'[11]

Through notices in the *North China Herald* of Horticultural Society prizewinners a picture emerges of the plants in the Ayscough garden: pansies, marguerites, iris, hydrangea, foxglove, begonia, sweet william, climbing nasturtiums, ferns. They also had a well-stocked vegetable garden producing prize-winning leeks, peas, onions and cauliflowers. They enjoyed particular success with chrysanthemums. In the Society's 1912 Autumn Flower Show, Florence won prizes for her 'Single Cream', 'Red Needle with Olea Center' and 'Pink Needle'. Francis' efforts were especially pioneering: 'Amongst the new varieties of chrysanthemum those shown by Mr. F. Ayscough attracted attention, having been grown from seeds brought from England. The experiment was novel and the excellence of the blooms was evidence of much success.'[12]

Shanghailander gardeners used a mixture of plants non-native and native to China—many of the latter had been transplanted into European gardens and became commonly thought of as thoroughly European, especially once European breeders developed new variants. When these were reintroduced into Chinese gardens by Western settlers, they ironically invoked nostalgia for home. An ecstatic review of the spring flowers at Jessfield Park (now Zhongshan Park), created in 1914 by the Municipal Council to the west of the Settlement, opined that the China rose had been 'vastly improved by selection and crossing at home' before being reintroduced to China. The familiarity of the plantings turned a trip to Jessfield Park into an evocation of home: 'The air is laden with the perfume of a million roses and at every turn of the Rose Garden fresh visions of England's own flower present themselves in a riot of colour.'[13]

As a cherished facet of Shanghailander culture, gardening was a means to recreate a patch of Hampstead or New Hampshire on the alluvial soil of Shanghai. Judging from the books and newspaper columns dedicated to gardening in Shanghai, it was an arena in which those with estates, or spacious grounds, or modest strips in front of lane houses, or even balcony planters, could animatedly discourse on seed catalogues, grafting, staking, pruning, and pests. In general, the ideal proffered was a trim, weed-free lawn, herbaceous borders brimming with familiar perennials, and beds of favourite annuals, calculated to evoke nostalgia in the hearts of even those for whom 'home' in the sense of permanent residence, had only ever been China: 'May is the month when our Shanghai gardens remind us most of England for Hollyhock, Lilac, Canterbury Bell and Sweet William now put on their brightest colours and recall to each of us sojourners in Shanghai the house where he was born.'[14]

The climate and soil conditions of the Yangtze Delta though, are quite different from those of the Home Counties; even when they imported seeds from Britain, Shanghai gardeners had to contend with heavy soil that rotted the roots of plants that pre-ferred well-aerated, friable earth; pervasive pampas grass; bamboo whose rhizomatous root systems formed intractable underground grids. The labour employed to wrestle with these conditions was provided by the much vilified Chinese gardener: 'As a class there is not a more unsatisfactory lot of men amongst the natives.'[15] In addition to laziness, slovenliness and ignorance, they were accused of pilfering and wanton negligence.

The more enlightened sojourners, though, understood that— aside from the obvious challenges of replicating a foreign garden-ing style in sometimes unsuitable conditions—other problems lay in lack of training for unskilled labourers, coupled with illiteracy. As Superintendant of Parks and Gardens, Donald MacGregor created a private school for trainee gardeners which taught basic gardening and literacy skills. Unfortunately due to a lack of finan-cial support, the school had closed by 1915. At the Horticultural Society's Annual General Meeting that year, Francis Ayscough, who was presiding in place of Sir Havilland de Sausmarez, made a plea for private donations to reinstate the school, arguing the importance of lifting men from illiteracy. He also cannily appealed to Shanghailanders' self-interest: 'I feel after long residence in

Shanghai how much horticulture and floriculture have done for the place … our parks, municipal roads, country clubs, private gardens, etc. all testify to what men and women have done and can do to beautify what was an unattractive spot in China.'[16]

In terms of aesthetics, his claims are unabashedly Eurocentric, and there was certainly an aspect of the Horticultural Society that privileged Western ideals. For Shanghailanders, the Society's flower shows offered a place to indulge tastes more Edwardian than Eastern. A typical tableau was the Shanghai Nursery's exhibit in 1907 comprising a lady's boa made of cornflowers, a muff of white carnations and tea roses, and parasol of springy green willow and roses.[17] Florence's floral arrangements, noted by *Social Shanghai*, were generally more tastefully subdued: 'A beautifully light and airy effect was attained by Mrs. Ayscough and Mrs. Wheelock who had arranged single pink chrysanthemums and asparagus fern in a series of irregular chrystal tubes. A linen and lace table centre was used, and stands of asparagus fern added to the ephemeral appearance of this pretty table.'[18]

However, the Society was also a place where Chinese horticultural knowledge could be shared, and where Chinese could participate beside other Asians and Europeans. Published lists of prizewinners attest to their prowess. In summer 1922, when Florence was receiving prizes for her begonias and Canterbury bells, Chinese growers were winning with their azaleas, tradescantia (spiderwort), and amaryllis. Mesdames Funatsu and Musakami and Miss Takada were awarded a prize for their Japanese garden, and Mrs. Funatsu, wife of the Japanese Consul General, was honoured for her decorated table.

By 1923 Florence had acquired enough knowledge of Chinese garden aesthetics to publish a lengthy scholarly article in Sowerby's prestigious *China Journal of Science and Arts*, and to create her own Chinese gardens for the Grass Hut. Her experiences with the Shanghai Horticultural Society must have provided some foundation for this, as well as her interactions with Donald MacGregor, who had created an experimental section in Jessfield Park for subtropical species. Here she could have studied the 2,000 shrubs brought from the nearby hill resort of Moganshan, plus collections of palms, bamboos and plane trees.[19]

Her activities with the Royal Asiatic Society would also have amplified her knowledge. The Society's journals are rich in Chinese botanical investigation. For example, sinologist Emil Bretschneider had published his encyclopedic *Botanicon Sinicum: Notes on Chinese Botany from Native and Western Sources* in a three-part series between 1881 and 1895.[20] Ayscough later referenced Bretschneider in her translations of Tu Fu.

But Ayscough was never one to confine herself to the library. She learned about gardens through visiting them, and about plants by observing them grow. She went to the Horticultural Society shows in the Town Hall and in the French Park (now Fuxing Park) as well as the Race Club, but she also went to the Chinese growers' competitions in the Chinese Old City. She observed the reverence with which they treated the *lan hua* orchid—the understated cymbidium with a fugitive scent and flecks of petals delitescent in foliage. To uncultivated eyes it was eclipsed by more showy tropical orchids, but to Chinese connoisseurs it was symbolic in its subtlety of the Confucian ideal of a gentleman or woman. During the *lan hua* season, Ayscough watched boats piled with cymbidium gathered from the hillsides floating along the waterways. As with European tulipomania during the seventeenth century, the pursuit of novelty, the hope of procuring a new striation or variation in colour incited Chinese speculators to purchase boatloads. She visited peony and azalea shows in the Old City, and observed the fragrant and expressive Buddha's Hand citrus, resting on rice or fine white sand in precious bowls. She understood that Europeans and Chinese thought about plants differently.

At a time when classical Chinese gardens were misunderstood and largely ignored by foreigners, and sometimes left to decay by Chinese, she visited and photographed the gardens of the southern Chinese cities once famed for their horticulture, such as Suzhou, Hangzhou and Nanjing. She photographed their neglect, and rejoiced in the conservation of sites such as Suzhou's Lion Grove Garden. Assisted by her teacher Nung Chu, who helped locate Chinese source material, she investigated the history of Shanghai's Yu Garden (Yuyuan)—the remnant of the exquisite sixteenth-century garden within the Old City. Through the decades this garden had suffered periods of destruction and neglect, and in 1919 was again endangered when the land was put up for auction. According to the *North China Herald* few foreigners even knew of its existence at this time: 'There were very few Europeans who, passing the white gate in Yu Yuen Road, ever knew of the delightful retreat that Chinese had built there ... The other morning the only admirers of the place were a foreigner and a kingfisher.'[21] Even as late as 1934 the guidebook *All About Shanghai and Environs* accorded the garden one brief sentence.

Florence, though, knew intimately every peeling corridor, solitary courtyard and reedy pond of the Yuyuan. She witnessed the disappearance of prized rocks, and efforts at repair and restoration. She enjoyed the ebullience of local holidays when the Shanghainese were admitted free of charge to clamber over the rockeries, and the eloquence of silent passageways and carved doorways framing emptiness. She was able to experience the Yuyuan and other southern gardens in a way almost always denied to visitors now that they have become major tourist attractions—as collections of spatial compositions, shifting, rearranging themselves as the visitor walks through them. She photographed and analysed them in her article in the *China Journal*, and based the design of her garden at the Grass Hut on principles she had learnt through her studies. She understood that although these gardens might seem repetitive or formulaic to Westerners, they were in fact deeply autobiographical, expressing the learning of their creators and owners, containing carefully curated collections of plants, rocks, quotations, artworks and books.

The footprint of her property, once Wild Goose Happiness House was sold, was very modest (her pug Yo Fei mourned the loss of the lawns he had once raced over). However, what she was able to create there was a retreat whose garden compositions in miniature suggested spacious landscapes, with collections of trees and flowers long cultivated in China and cherished for their symbolic, literary and medicinal properties. Snaking around the east of the property, in a nod to the Yuyuan, was a noble-headed dragon wall. Inside the first court were 'hills' of water-worn rocks specially selected by Ayscough and artfully arranged by an elderly connoisseur (*Figure 9*). A path wound up an azalea-covered 'mountain' to a temple housing a stone on which Nung Chu had written 'spirit' (another reference to the Yuyuan's shrine to the spirit of the hills). Initially Ayscough had planned a perfectly round moon gate, just as she had photographed in the Yuyuan, at the end of a pebbled path, but a 'misunderstanding' turned it into an oval. This led to a bamboo grove intended to be 'perfectly wild … as if one stepped out to the mountain-side, peopled only by spirits of the dead.'[22] Heaped flower-sown earth simulated the ubiquitous grave mounds found in all such places. Other 'spirits of the dead' were contained in a small spirit tablet house, specially built by the Ayscoughs to house the generations of 'intangible wraiths' residing in stone

Figure 9 Lucille Douglass, drawing of garden at 72 Penang Road. From *A Chinese Mirror*.

tablets inconveniently forgotten by the property's previous owners. These orphans were adopted by the Ayscoughs' household staff who ensured that acceptable sacrifices were offered at the right times.

Another suggested landscape was composed just inside the entrance photographed for Florence's 1934 Christmas card. Plum trees, pines and bamboos were grouped around a waterfall that descended into a fish pool bordered by the prized native medicinal plant 'ten thousand years green' (*rohdea japonica*). Scattered around, representing an ancient palace in the wilderness, were shards of broken tiles glinting turquoise, yellow, mauve and green, salvaged by Ayscough from the ruins of the Yuanmingyuan, or the old Summer Palace, in Beijing, sacked by British and French troops in 1860.

These small gardens were a showcase for treasured plants, such as a tuberous-rooted grass she identified as 'book girdle grass'. This had been a gift from 'a lonely, miserable old tailor who sewed in the back quarters for years' and was laden with literary significance, as well as being an effective remedy for haemorrhage. Other species with long histories as Chinese garden plants included the powerfully scented osmanthus, a paulownia heavy with purple blossom, woody-scented azalea, and the evergreen Chinese cinnamon. In bloom, the magnolia blossoms glowed white against the weathered charcoal roof tiles. An old gnarled pine 'like a Buddhist priest or a Taoist' provided the requisite gravity. When Ayscough initially selected a pliant young pine, Nung Chu had corrected her with 'pity and tolerant patience'.

For a Shanghailander to create a Chinese garden that demonstrated understanding of Chinese garden aesthetics and the meanings of plants was highly unusual. Surviving photographs and descriptions show that it was not rare for Shanghai gardens belonging to foreigners to have Chinese statuary or areas dedicated to *chinoiserie* with pavilions, zigzag bridges, carp pools and lotus ponds. The forward-thinking writer Lin Yutang bemoaned the uninformed and incongruous adoption of Chinese motifs by Shanghai residents who paid hundreds of thousands of dollars to purchase a modest lot. 'Once they get to that point, they proceed to bulldoze it flat, trim the greenery into pyramids, cones, and other three-dimensional shapes, form flower-beds in strange geometric patterns, and construct five-foot-high artificial mountains and seven-foot-wide fish ponds. Having accomplished all of this, they seem immensely pleased with themselves. It's a sight to wrench one's heart.'[23]

Unkaza, the spectacular estate of early Shanghailander Edward Jenner Hogg, had been built on an old temple site, and had two stone horses from an official's grave facing the house.[24] It was a portion of the Unkaza Estate that was sold in 1914 to become Jessfield Park. On a much smaller scale Arthur de Carle Sowerby, Shanghai's leading foreign naturalist, had created a *chinoiserie*-inspired garden on Lucerne Road (now Lixi Road). An amalgam of Western and Chinese elements, this garden had a bridge with a Chinese shrine, a statue of the goddess Guanyin surrounded by ferns brought back from Moganshan, clumps of bamboos, green-glazed lions from a Beijing temple, and a rocky grotto with a brown porcelain Laughing Buddha.[25] Different again in character was Aili Garden, Shanghai's most sumptuous private garden built by Jewish property tycoon Silas Hardoon on Bubbling Well Road. Eight thousand guests could gather in the lush grounds, to enjoy the streams, rockeries and lakes, the collections of Chinese plants, and the hidden pagodas and teahouses.[26] Aili Garden, though, was on an entirely different scale from the Grass Hut garden, and had been designed by a Buddhist monk who acted as advisor to Hardoon and his Buddhist Eurasian wife Luo Jialing. What differentiated Ayscough's garden was that it was a unique attempt by a Westerner to understand and express an entire aesthetic approach (not just parts of vocabulary such as lion dogs or Buddha statues). Within the limited boundaries of her garden she concentrated the essence of what she understood of Chinese garden design—much as she and Lowell attempted to condense the spirit of Chinese poetry in their translations.

Just like the gardens of the Grass Hut, the buildings too were informed by her knowledge of Chinese aesthetics and were full of humour, idiosyncrasy and autobiography. She claimed that her new home was 'to be like the cottages of Kiangsu [Jiangsu, the province north and west of Shanghai], and … I want to observe all time-honoured customs while it is being built.' In her essay in *A Chinese Mirror* she describes the process of construction: the roles and activities of the workmen from senior foreman to young apprentice; the layout and decoration of the architectural elements; the design of the garden; and the decoration of the interior, explaining all the cultural contexts that influenced how these looked. For example, the action of raising the richly carved ridge pole—in many cultures the most portentous moment in the building of a home—was surrounded by ceremonies, singing, offerings to Lu Ban (the patron saint of carpenters,) and gift-giving. She explains the significance of every item laid before Lu Ban's effigy, in passages that go well beyond the merely descriptive, relying on her understanding of Chinese language, culture and history. For instance, she illustrates the much-exploited punning potential of the language through explaining that the herb 'ten thousand years green', which was tied to the ridge pole during the ceremony, was symbolic in that *qing* (green) sounds similar to *qing* (congratulate, celebrate). To Western readers of this account of elaborate protocol, this must have seemed a distant enigma—either an example of a fictitiously 'changeless' China, or a possibly romanticized description of archaic customs that couldn't endure far into the Republican era. However, today in regions even close to cosmopolitan Shanghai, the completion of a roof structure is celebrated with the same explosive firecrackers that Ayscough heard, and sometimes with bunches of grasses tied with red bindings to beams.

But for all its observance of tradition, the Grass Hut was first and foremost the home of a wealthy Western resident of Shanghai, conditioned to the privileges and conveniences entirely foreign to a rural retreat. In no way did Ayscough ever suggest to her readers that she had 'gone native'. On one page she writes 'I continually reiterate that it is to be like the cottages of Kiangsu', but on the next she includes a plan of a spacious and well-staffed home, with bath-rooms attached to each bedroom, a central heating furnace room, a smoking room and a pantry. She elaborates:

> It is difficult to preserve a completely Chinese interior when one must introduce that Occidental comfort of which I have already spoken. Fire-places for instance are entirely exotic to a Kiangsu cottage. I have tried to mitigate the delightful evil by framing ours in a flat round circle. Lights have been cleverly concealed by the electrician in old Chinese fittings. There are beautiful candelabra, and black iron hanging baskets formerly used to hold both flowers and candles. Bright silk tassels, yellow, green, purple and scarlet, hang from all light fixtures and the colours blend most effectively.

Light filtered softly through windows made of the linings of mussel shells, fitted into bamboo frames, perhaps inspired by an example in the Old City; in an essay on Shanghai's City God cult,

Florence had noted the loveliness of coloured light falling through the temple's pearl shell windows. The house was full of antiques she had collected in Shanghai and during trips to other provinces. Above the fireplace was an ink rubbing obtained in Sichuan during a trip along the Yangtze in the early summer of 1922 (*Figure 10*). A pair of Ming-dynasty black and gold lacquered cupboards graced the Guest Hall, along with Chinese chairs and tables. 'Occidental comfort', though, was supplied by overstuffed sofas and armchairs. Among scholar's treasures were a set of seals of rare 'chicken-blood stone' and a carved bamboo brush holder. From donations later made to museums, descriptions compiled by her second husband, and contemporary newspaper accounts it is possible to build up a picture of the Chinese antiques she had collected (though some items were added during subsequent trips back to China with Francis, and later Harley MacNair). In addition to paintings and ceramics she was greatly interested in textiles, and left some superb examples to North American museums, such as an early seventeenth-century panel gifted to the Art Institute of Chicago, in woven silk and gold leaf over lacquered-paper-strip-wrapped silk, depicting birds, butterflies, and flowers (*Plate 3*). Following Ayscough's death, MacNair's bequest to this museum in memory of his wife included textiles, ceramics, paintings, various artifacts from diverse historic periods, calligraphy and ink rubbings.[27]

In collecting textiles of this calibre, Ayscough belonged to a group of prominent (often female) foreign collectors in China, some of whom were procuring items for Western museums. These included Lucy Calhoun, one of Ayscough's companions during her 1922 Yangtze River trip. Calhoun was the wife of an American diplomat posted to Beijing, and the sister of Harriet Monroe, founder and editor of *Poetry*, the magazine in which several Ayscough/Lowell translations appeared before the publication of

Figure 10 Lucille Douglass, drawing of interior at) 2 Penang Road. From
A Chinese Mirror.

Fir-Flower Tablets. As a member of the Art Institute of Chicago's auxiliary organization the Antiquarian Society, Calhoun purchased fine quality pieces including eighteenth-and nineteenth-century imperial robes, a Ming-dynasty panel, and rare religious vestments.[28] Chinese textiles were of enough interest to be the subject of a Royal Asiatic Society talk in April 1913, by the curator of the Society's Museum, Dr. Stanley.[29] In his lecture he noted that foreigners were particularly fascinated by the intricacy of Chinese embroideries, and their often startling colour combinations—Lucy Calhoun had seen fit to warn the chair of the Antiquarian's purchasing committee of this characteristic.

Among Western collectors richly embroidered court textiles received most attention. But Ayscough was also drawn to Chinese regional textiles which were of far less appeal to foreigners, certainly at institutional level. She frequently wrote with admiration of the indigo-dyed clothing worn by farmers in the areas around Shanghai: 'It always seems to me a merciful dispensation of Providence that the people in China grow indigo and therefore dye their clothes such heavenly blues; what other colour would blend with the landscape so well?'[30] A gift later given to Beloit College, Wisconsin contains non-court clothing, as well as a few folk pieces, such as a blue and white wax-resist cotton baby's bib (*Plate 4*).

Ayscough could have obtained such items during her extensive trips within China; like many modern tourists she was capable of stopping people on the street and asking to buy their possessions. She later recounted, with shame, how she had tried to press a man into selling her his dog! Regional furniture such as a Yunnan screen with an insert of figured marble might have been purchased during travel in western China. Woodwork salvaged from an old house in Suzhou was retro-fitted into a display cabinet. Some items could have been purchased closer to home; Ayscough loved to rummage through the shops of the Old City of Shanghai, having a particular fondness for the tassel shop, with its wares ranging from fat, fecund wedding-bed tassels to delicately-wrought ornaments for birdcages. She was also much attached to the coffin shop, admiring the glossy black-lacquered coffins, grave clothes, soul banners and spirit tablets. It was likely in the streets of the Old City that she procured the signboards that baffled members of the American Women's Club at a talk she hosted at her home. Among the rare porcelain, jades, and an ivory comb which had belonged to the Empress Dowager were 'some strange looking old printing boards which Mrs. Ayscough said, were placards advertising the wares of a vegetable vendor', and some wrought iron pictures created by a blacksmith.[31]

In *A Chinese Mirror*, Ayscough's essay on the Grass Hut was illustrated by the American artist Lucille Douglass (1876–1935). By the time Douglass arrived in China in 1920, she had established a career as a professional artist, though Ayscough's subsequent patronage and support was to help secure her financial position as a self-supported artist and lecturer. Having received a Bachelor's degree in art from the Alabama Female College, she continued to study in New York at the Art Students League and in Europe. She was working in New York when she was invited by the Board of Foreign Missions of the Methodist Episcopal Church to organize a slide-colouring department in China.[32] She swiftly established a workshop at 4 Quinsan Gardens (on what is now Tanggu Road), an area of diverse Christian missionary activity. The workshop employed Chinese adolescent girls and built up a library of slides for the mission's use in lectures throughout China. When Douglass accepted this position, she stipulated that work opportunities be given to Chinese women, because of 'her constant interest in the feminist movement'. While employed under Douglass, the girls learnt English and some received tuition fees to attend school. Her promotion of educational opportunities for Chinese women would certainly have found empathy with Ayscough, whom she probably met in November 1921 when Douglass was lecturing to the American Women's Club.[33] Soon the workshop was creating hand-coloured slides for Ayscough.

Ayscough's lectures were becoming performances. She was often dressed in Chinese robes, and reviews in newspapers repeatedly stressed that her talks were beautifully illustrated, often with hand-coloured lantern slides produced from her own photographs. For Ayscough, having her slides meticulously hand-coloured by Douglass' workshop ensured that the subjects were presented as realistically as possible. At first Douglass as an artist bridled against Ayscough's 'absolutely undeviating devotion to the truth', as she explained in an introduction to *Firecracker Land*: 'This unswerving loyalty on her part and my artistic impressionism often brought me in sharp contact with unexpected corners. This same divergence of viewpoint was introduced when I was painting the slides for her lecture on Tu Fu. I looked at them from the pictorial angle, she from the point of the incident she wished to illustrate.'[34] These slides must have been a superb photographic record of China's landscapes, religious and tourist sites and popular customs during the early Republic period. After Ayscough's death Harley MacNair gifted her slide collection to the China Society of New York,[35] but to date, this valuable material remains untraced. A small collection of slides picturing Amy Lowell at Sevenels, though, belongs to Harvard University.[36]

Her written works often mention her practice of photography, and some of her writing is accompanied by her own photographs. Some of her subjects were those favoured by many Western amateur photographers—especially people and landscapes. She was a voracious photographer of people, photographing her neighbours and workmen, and once, at a Chinese New Year party at the Grass Hut in 1927 she photographed 200 of her former employees and their families. She photographed landscapes, some of which were transformed by Douglass into the pen and ink drawings to illustrate her essays in *A Chinese Mirror*. She was especially pleased with her photographs taken during her 1922 Yangtze trip; before they departed from Yichang, a heavy rainfall had swollen the river, 'so all the cascades were full of water and made the most extraordinary effect as they were every imaginable shade of colour from a deep blood-red, through deep copper, and light copper, to gold, straw colour, and pure sparkling white.'[37] She hoped to send these photographs to Douglass so the artist could capture these colours through hand painting. Some of her photographs survive in archives, such as a small collection of gelatin silver prints of Japanese gardens, taken during a visit to Japan in 1927 with Mary Matteson Wilbur (*Figure 11*). Mary Wilbur (1872–1957) had been one of Ayscough's closest friends for many years. With her husband Hollis Wilbur, secretary to the YMCA, she lived in Japan, Korea and China for 40 years. The two women were faithful correspondents, and surviving letters help flesh out the details of Ayscough's life after leaving China.

Many of her photographs and slides were probably ethnographic; she was fascinated by the indigenous religion practised through the cult of the City God in Shanghai, and Douglass' drawings for her essay in *A Chinese Mirror* depict traditional observances such as the shoe-shaped paper ingots burnt in offering to the city's Spiritual Magistrates. Most of these were probably drawn from Ayscough's photographs, which she would have used in her talk on the subject to the Royal Asiatic Society in London in 1924. She may have habitually carried a camera with her, not only for

Figure 11 Florence Ayscough, gelatin silver print on paper, of a park or temple site, Japan, 1927. Schlesinger Library, Radcliffe Institute, Harvard University.

fieldwork, but for everyday chance encounters. During one of their daily walks in the countryside beyond Suzhou Creek, Ayscough and Yo Fei came across a traditional funeral cortege of white-clad mourners riding on wheelbarrows, 'like a silver serpent undulating across the fields'.[38] Wanting to capture the spectacle on film, Ayscough raced from furrow to furrow, inciting the admiration of a surprised mourner: 'she *can* gallop'. This wasn't the only time she stretched herself in pursuit of a good shot; when she received an Honorary D.Litt. from Acadia University, Nova Scotia in 1927, she scrambled onto the roof of the gymnasium to get a better shot of University Hall; Douglass then created an edition of etchings after the photograph, which were sold by the University.[39]

For Ayscough, photography wasn't an artistic or expressive tool, but, as Douglass makes clear, a means to record reality. She may have seen her photographic work in contrast to the popular and widely disseminated studio shots that perpetuated anachronistic ideas about China, or the equally popular, often staged, and sometimes ghoulish explorations of criminal behaviours, punishments, or eroticism. In contrast, her published photographs of, for example, Chinese gardens are unromanticized, undidactic, and unassuming. They show tangles of overgrown wisteria vine, reed-choked verges and bamboos overhanging waterways. Soon, she would explore how photography could be put to service in illustrating new scholarship—such as her archeological reinterpretations on Guernsey.

After China

Holding Open the Door

In April 1923 the Ayscoughs sailed away from Shanghai, arriving in St. Andrews, New Brunswick in May. They intended to make Topside, the house Thomas Wheelock had built in 1897, their permanent home. They brought with them 43 cases of household goods. These held some of the antique collection Florence had been building for decades; a photograph of Ayscough in the Topside drawing room shows her posed with her arm on a Chinese armchair, one of the jars given to her by Empress Dowager Cixi in the foreground. They also held her books and papers; when she wrote to Lowell soon after arriving in St. Andrews, these were what she was most eager to unpack. Before leaving China she had been working assiduously on a major translation of Tu Fu's poetry. Her trip along the Yangtze River the year before had been a homage to the poet who had produced so much of his stark late poetry in Kuizhou, a river town in the Yangtze Gorges where he had lived from 766 to 768. She had visited what was identified as his home, where he had found a hiatus of tranquility in the midst of a turbulent life: 'We had a hard time finding it and were led by a man in a bright blue turban (the Szechuanese, generally speaking, wear turbans—most picturesque) up Moon's Tooth Street, high up the hill to the city wall before we arrived at our destination.'[1] As always, she wanted to ground her work in personal experience. Tracing Tu Fu's steps, she read his poems *in situ*; the sensory experience of place that underpinned *Fir-Flower Tablets* was to infuse her 'auto-biography' of Tu Fu—the two volumes of translations that have been an enduring contribution to scholarship. Along the gorges she experienced the soaking mists and pervasive smell of rain that allowed her to translate the feeling of this watery, shifting, turbu-lent place:

> In chasms   when daylight   comes,   clouds   drive;
> Mists,   scuds,   waft back   and forth   together.
>
> Squally   wind   blows down   cold   river;
> Pattering   raindrops   bounce   from rock   cliffs.[2]

She hoped to work again with Lowell on the Tu Fu project, but Lowell was absorbed in her own monumental 1,300-page biog-raphy of John Keats. In addition to labouring on translation, Ayscough began to devote much energy to maintaining a life rooted in St. Andrews, but with winter migrations to Europe. In St. Andrews she and Frank sailed their sloop *Wu Yuen*, accompa-nied by Yo Fei, tucked in his striped sweater against the salty wind. The little dog had been left in Shanghai in 1923, but had pined so badly that he was crated and sent in the hold of a steamship to Canada where Florence had to revive the shivering, emaciated creature with whipped egg whites. He recovered, and learnt to endure the water that was so much the character of the Canadian Maritimes. Like golf, sailing ran in the family—Thomas Wheelock had sailed several craft in St. Andrews, including a custom-made 42-foot yacht and an 18½-foot yawl. Francis and Florence watched whales in the Passamaquoddy Bay, and hiked the trails they'd cut through the spruce and balsam on their private island, visible in the bay from the windows of Topside. They gardened, tending the borders around the sweep of lawn, and perhaps experimenting with plants grown in Shanghai (*Plate 5*). Florence immersed herself in Canadian literary life, lectured locally on Chinese topics, and in 1926 donated the Niger Reef Tea House to the Passamaquoddy Chapter of the Imperial Order Daughters of the Empire.[3] Her friend and collaborator Lucille Douglass came out to New Brunswick, and painted the tea house's interior murals.

Winters were spent in England and Continental Europe. Florence was becoming an increasingly sought-after speaker at scholarly and literary venues. In January 1924 she wrote to Lowell from Berkshire; she had just lectured before the Royal Asiatic Society of Great Britain and Ireland, and was much gratified to have been praised by eminent sinologist Herbert A. Giles. She was shortly to speak to the China Society and the Lyceum Club, then on to another engagement in Guernsey, home of her close friends Sir Havilland and Lady de Sausmarez, who had retired from China in 1921.[4] An escape to a more clement climate, and the wish to participate in an expanded cultural life motivated these annual decampments, but more critically, the Ayscoughs were searching for a diagnosis and cure for Francis' illness. When she wrote to Lowell in spring 1924 there was brief hope that they had found a skilled doctor 'who has done Frank a lot of good. He is a different person which is an immense comfort.'[5] Whatever physical symptoms he suffered, his emotional well-being and morale were deeply eroded—a circumstance that was to bring Florence herself great suffering. The decade from 1923 to 1933 was filled with professional achievement, but also with emotional difficulty and loss.

Putting aside Tu Fu while she waited for Lowell to complete her biography of Keats, she published other texts that seem to have come more easily. *A Chinese Mirror* (1925) was compiled from lectures she had delivered in China and London, including three to the North China Branch of the Royal Asiatic Society. The next year she produced *The Autobiography of a Chinese Dog*, which, purportedly from the perspective of Yo Fei, reminisced about life in Weihaiwei—the British lease on the Shandong peninsula where Florence and her family had spent several summers—and the rhythms of household life at 60 Gordon Road. Both books were illustrated by Lucille Douglass. She also wrote a brief catalogue for Douglass' exhibition of pastels, *Waterways of China*, exhibited at the Anderson Galleries, New York in spring 1925. Her books and lectures were well received; she was popularly considered 'brilliant', and a reliable crowd pleaser; she was also acknowledged as authoritative. In 1921 the North China Branch of the Royal Asiatic Society had elected her to the position of 'Honorary Member'. She was the first woman to receive this title, and took her place among sinologists such as Herbert A. Giles, Henri Cordier, Paul Pelliot, and Sir J. H. Stewart Lockhart.[6] In 1926 she was elected to the Society of Woman Geographers.[7] In 1927 she was elected a member of the Royal Geographical Society[8] while Acadia University in Nova Scotia awarded her an Honorary D. Litt. the same year.[9]

Frank's illness, though, took a toll that was only properly acknowledged to close friends. Amy Lowell died suddenly in 1925; afterwards Ayscough suffered a loneliness that often expressed itself in self-doubt. During the production of *Fir-Flower Tablets* the two friends had rallied around each other; Lowell's bombast had been quite sufficient to shore up any latent crises of confidence. By the mid-1920s Ayscough had lost her closest friend and also, inexorably, the companionship and camaraderie of her husband. When in 1925 she lectured in French in Paris—'a truly terrifying prospect for one as retiring as myself'—Frank did not accompany her. Despite their earlier decision to winter in Shanghai, his apprehension about the deteriorating political situation kept them away until the winter of 1926—hardly a propitious time for a trip to China.

In May 1925, the month Ayscough memorialized Lowell in the dedication to *A Chinese Mirror* (a book that eulogized Chinese traditions at their most peaceful and enduring), Shanghai erupted into paralyzing demonstrations and strikes. The trouble culminated in the International Settlement on 30 May, when police under British command fired on a crowd of unarmed anti-imperialist workers and students. The ensuing violence ricocheted throughout China, stoking an increasingly aggressive anti-foreign nationalism that searched for expression in organized political action. The Guomindang—the Nationalist Party—and the recently formed Chinese Communist Party united, for a while, in the goal of unifying China; by the time of the Ayscoughs' visit, however, the alliance had fractured and Shanghai had become a site of contest. Outside Shanghai the Nationalists were pursuing a savage campaign to recapture provinces fought over by warlords. By December 1926 they controlled seven provinces: Guangdong, Hunan, Hubei, Jiangxi, Fujian, Guangxi and Guizhou, and were pushing with unnerving rapidity northwards towards the Yangtze. Why the Ayscoughs chose to stay in Shanghai throughout the winter and into the volatile spring of 1927 is explained perhaps by foreigners' belief in the Nationalists' assurance of their immunity, and in their own firepower; by spring there were 22,000 foreign troops and police in the city, backed up by 42 warships.

On Florence's part, there was her self-acknowledged stubbornness, bravura, and curiosity. In a letter to Mary Wilbur that appears to date from this visit, Florence expresses all three, as well as an understandable scintilla of anxiety: 'I trust there will not be any

bles"—My husband is not keen to experience them!! Neither
I, for the matter of fact, but I am more ready I think than he is
ake my share of discomfort—I mean as I am more interested I
l more responsibility in accepting what comes!'[10]

In early spring 1927, while the Nationalists were preparing to
nter Shanghai from the south, and foreign troops were turning
the city into a garrison, Florence was gamely lecturing in French on
Chinese gardens at the French Club. Harley MacNair was among
the audience, and as he recollected, Florence continued to lecture
when the building was struck by stray shellfire. But Florence
'without a tremor in her voice, again, requested the pleasure of
the meeting. Several Frenchmen, not to be outdone in gallantry
by a woman, or a British subject, assured her of their continued
interest—and Florence composedly finished her lecture.'[11]

On 21 March 1927 Shanghai erupted into vicious insurrec-
tion directed by the Chinese Communist Party, in support of the
advancing Nationalists. Troops entered the city the next day. For
a few short weeks an uneasy Nationalist–Communist alliance
sought to tread between the opposing interests of the trade unions,
industrialists, financiers, gangsters and racketeers. Inevitably,
consensus was an impossibility. On 12 April a bloody purge of the
Communists began, sanctioned by the Guomindang leadership,
and in part assisted by the foreign authorities. When Florence felt
the first shell thud into the walls of the French Club, she must have
understood that the foreign enclave of Shanghai was not immuta-
ble. When her friend the author Alice Tisdale Hobart almost lost
her life during the Nationalist occupation of Nanjing, she must
have accepted that foreign lives and property were not sacrosanct.
It was time to leave Shanghai.

Back in St. Andrews N.B., she continued working on Tu
Fu, whose own weary experience of the chaos and famine that

accompanied political turmoil made him such an iconic anti-war poet. After the Shanghai spring, she must have understood.

> The State is destroyed; hills, rivers remain;
> Spring: within the city wall, grass, trees, are thick.
> Emotion, fitting to the season; flowers bring a rush of tears;
> I hate being cut apart; the song of birds quickens my heart.[12]

She wrote to her friend John Livingston Lowes, Coleridge scholar and professor of English literature at Harvard, acknowledging the gift of his recent book. The regret behind her comment, 'how Amy would have loved it' was reinforced by the extraordinary confession: 'I feel far more intimate with Tu Fu—he died in 780 AD—than I do with anyone living. I mean that quite literally.'[13] Tu Fu, though, was an exigent companion. She had started translating this poet nearly a decade earlier. She had spent the tense winter of 1926–27 studying daily with Nung Chu, deciphering his words, excavating his life. She told Lowes she had translated 800 to 1000 of his poems. As with many biographers, she was stunned by the 'mass' of material she had accumulated, and unsure how to craft it into a book: 'It is quite impossible for me to express to you how utterly inadequate I feel before this task, this monument, this what shall I call it?' In part it was a problem of quantity; she was working with an edition of 21 'limp, closely printed Chinese booklets'. In part though, it was a problem of what audience to pitch this erudite work to. She was a speaker accustomed to drawing standing-room-only crowds, and her publications were admired for their accessibility as well as authority, but now she confided, 'I do not see how I am to condense the material within reasonable bounds and then am I going to find people who will be sufficiently interested to read pages and pages about a man of whom they have never heard, even if I succeed in making it "live"." A French friend had called the popular *Chinese Mirror* 'un travail de vulgarisation', and now implored her not to make Tu Fu 'trop petit'.

She continued onwards, through 1927 and 1928, translating, lecturing, and also writing a long introduction to Alice Tisdale Hobart's *Within the Walls of Nanking*—Hobart's taut, personal account of the Nationalists' advance on Nanjing in 1927, and the killing of Chinese and foreign civilians. Hobart had endured a terrifying escape over the city walls on ropes, and a harrowing race through sniper-infested darkness to the safety of foreign gunboats. The example of Nanjing undermined foreigners' perception of their personal invulnerability. Ayscough's introduction was a historical orientation to 'the ancient structure which China has discarded', but she was in part motivated by a desire to enlighten a self-absorbed Western audience about the upheaval in contemporary China. They had great trouble securing a publisher, and she observed sadly to Mary Wilbur in January 1928, 'Fewer people seem to care about China.'[14] Ayscough was absorbed in other preoccupations, though. By now, Francis' condition was rapidly deteriorating. He was ill the entire winter of 1927–8, and 'very miserable'.[15]

Tu Fu: The Autobiography of a Chinese Poet was at last published in 1929; far from being *trop petit*, its 450 pages traced the poet's life through his poetry from AD 712 to 759. Although some of Ayscough's chronology has since been revised, it was still a remarkable achievement. It would take another five years for Ayscough to complete the second volume of the poet's story. The Shanghai Library holds copies of both volumes of the *Autobiography*; in her elegant handwriting in purple ink they are inscribed to Lin Yutang, the Chinese writer whose own prodigious publications later helped explain China to the West. Tu Fu's *Autobiography* is rich in Ayscough's own memories of China, the landscape and climate, and the days and years spent with Nung Chu. Tu Fu travels, marries, holds office, resigns, wanders, experiences war and famine, and writes; Ayscough and Nung Chu study, converse, write, and like Tu Fu they drink straw-coloured sweet chrysanthemum tea, 'a liquid link … down the centuries'.[16] Compared with *Fir-Flower Tablets*, these translations are sparser, and far less explanatory. For example, dispirited by autumn rain, Tu Fu notices the resilience of the marsh plant *chueh ming* [Chinese senna, or sicklepod]:

> Drenched in autumn rain, one hundred plants rot, die;
> Below the steps, however, your colour, *chüeh ming*, is fresh
> Bright fine leaves crowd your stalk, feathery, grass like, kingfisher green;
> Your flowers in bloom, yellow gold like coins, are few.[17]

This was a bittersweet time for Ayscough; the critical success of the *Autobiography* affirmed her stature as an internationally respected scholar. The *Journal of the Royal Asiatic Society of Great Britain and Ireland* applauded the 'lucid and simple writing which will give even the uninitiated a genuine idea of the feeling and form of the Chinese lines'.[18] She had herself become an assiduous book reviewer for this journal. She continued to enjoy popular success too, appearing as a guest on A. M. Sullivan's *The New Poetry Hour* on WOR Radio, New York.[19] (She would later be featured in a Fox film, writing calligraphy and talking about Chinese characters in German.[20]) Dating from 1929 is a portrait drawing she may herself have commissioned, by the English artist William Rothenstein (*Figure 12*). In being represented by this portraitist of literary

Figure 12 Florence Ayscough, portrait drawing by William Rothenstein, 1929. Special Collections Research Center, University of Chicago Library. Copyright the artist's estate/Bridgeman Art Library.

giants and artists, Ayscough took her place beside Hardy, Eliot, Einstein, Shaw, and Rodin. But 1929 was also the year in which the Ayscoughs left St. Andrews, for the peripatetic years until Francis' death.

While her husband sought treatment in Vienna, Florence attempted to continue her scholarship, though she sorely missed her home and garden. She wrote in November 1930 to Wilbur:

> My husband I am sorry to say is in a sanatorium near by and is much as he was. I am beginning to feel that his is a problem which cannot be solved and must, in the words of Jung, be 'overgrown', that is I must arrange things so that he is as comfortable as may be and then try to carry on my own affairs with as little disturbance as possible. This gypsy life is hardly one which I would choose, but I am becoming very expert at folding myself and my belongings into an hotel room, and of course there are certain advantages such as facility of travel connected with the life.[21]

She recounted to Wilbur that she had lectured in Berlin and Stockholm, where she caught up with her old friend and colleague the Scandinavian art historian Osvald Sirén. The two scholars shared an interest in Chinese gardens in addition to Chinese art; Sirén was to bring out his own landmark publication in 1948, translated into English the next year as *Gardens of China*. Both scholars were keen documentary photographers. Ayscough in the past had helped Sirén with translations from the Chinese, and back in 1924 there had been a tentative plan to co-write a book on Chang'an (the Tang-dynasty capital city, now Xi'an).[22] By 1930 there was no further word on this, probably because of the uncertainty in Ayscough's personal life. But, as she wrote to Wilbur, she was resolvedly industrious. She had her car, and motored extensively throughout Central Europe. She was about to leave for Darmstadt, and the following January she was to travel to the United States on a lecture tour. Relentless activity rubs the edges off grief. In March 1931, while Florence was travelling across America, Francis had his right leg amputated because of gangrene.[23] Remarkably, the operation 'improved his morale very greatly', she explained to Wilbur. 'He is of course weak and helpless but so much happier than he has been for years.'[24]

As soon as Francis was well enough to travel the couple moved to Guernsey. The Channel Islands' clement climate, the companionship of Havilland and Annie de Sausmarez, proximity to Francis' family in England, and the ability to establish a coastal home once more with a spacious garden, all motivated this move. Having lived all her life on plains or by the sea, Florence was tired of mountains, and was seeking another home where she could, as she told Amy Lowell's long-time partner Ada Russell, feel in harmony with herself. The house she purchased in the summer of 1931 was 22 Hauteville, St. Peter Port, on the Channel Island of Guernsey. It was an elegant five-storey house that shared a common wall with what had once been the home of Victor Hugo's mistress Juliette Drouet—a fact that Ayscough seemed rather to enjoy. The high-walled fruit and flower gardens faced the sea, and from her bedroom above, Florence could imagine herself 'suspended between sky and sea'.[25] The extensive formal gardens of Sausmarez Manor must also have given her immense pleasure, especially as the mild climate allowed the cultivation of plants long familiar from Shanghai gardening days: bamboo, palm, camellia, rhododendron, azalea.

In addition to caring for Francis—gangrene necessitated the amputation of his left leg later in 1931—Florence immediately submerged herself in the history of this archeologically rich island, with its prehistoric standing stones, iron-age fortifications, medieval churches and Georgian architecture. She continued to explore photography as a documentary tool, providing the photographs for explorer Ralph Durand's *Guernsey Past and Present* (1933). She became especially interested in the island's enigmatic megaliths and created a method of floodlighting them at night, running muslin-covered spotlights on long flexes from her car. Her wide-angled lens and ten-minute exposures threw carvings into relief, uncovered unsuspected symbols, and excavated the expressions of deities, provoking new hypotheses that she would present in publications and lectures. She had a fertile mind much appreciated by British archeologists, but also a flair for frivolity. In the midst of a meeting of the International Congress of Prehistoric and Protohistoric Sciences, after she had delivered her own paper, she felt suddenly oppressed by the drabness and stale erudition and bolted to London's most expensive hat shop to assuage her ennui.[26]

Francis died on 6 December 1933, at Beechwood Nursing Home, St. Peter Port. The causes of death were listed as endarteritis obliterans and cerebral thrombosis (stroke).[27] The diagnosis explains Francis' excruciating last decade; the first condition is an autoimmune disease affecting the circulation and leading to constant pain, ulceration and gangrene, as well as neurosis. Both Francis and Florence had suffered a great deal since leaving Shanghai, where Francis had been a vigorous sportsman, genial companion, advocate for the respect of ponies and self-improvement of gardeners. Florence's memorial to her husband is a testament to his happier nature. In the church of St. James the Great, Cradley, where Francis' father had been Rector for 25 years, is a glowing, opalescent stained-glass window by A. J. Davies of the eminent Arts and Crafts workshop The Bromsgove Guild. It depicts the gentle, cheerful, nature-loving St. Francis of Assisi in a garden, surrounded by birds and animals (*Plate 6*). It is dedicated by Florence Ayscough, to the 'dear memory' of Francis and his parents.

Despite the travail, and the moments when 'the depression—but it should have a capital "D"—simply stalks', Florence continued to work steadily on part two of Tu Fu.[28] *Travels of a Chinese Poet: Tu Fu, Guest of Rivers and Lakes* was published the next year in June, by which time she had returned to Shanghai. She had arrived in spring, in time to lecture at the end of the Royal Asiatic Society's season in their splendid new art-deco building on Museum Road behind the Bund Florence had known so well. She explained her return to John Livingston Lowes:

> I felt I must come back and see New China and try to orient myself anew. Whether I stay here permanently or not remains to be seen. My plan is to remain for a year at least … It is difficult to adjust oneself to a life wherein the only responsibilities are to oneself—that is, if one has been accustomed for many years to quite different conditions.[29]

Debilitated, probably, by the strain of the previous months, she contracted typhoid and spent the hot, humid summer in hospital (there are many hospitals marked on Dunlap's map of Shanghai; Shanghailanders founded them, were treated in them, and as indicated in the newspaper obituaries, frequently died in them). When she recovered, she received a visit from an old friend, Harley Farnsworth MacNair. Since first meeting Ayscough in the library of the Royal Asiatic Society in 1916, MacNair, 16 years her junior, had been in love with her.[30] Over the interceding two decades, in Shanghai, St. Andrews, Guernsey and Chicago, his subconscious courtship was expressed, very properly and respectfully, through deep friendship, and the discussion of Chinese history, travel and books.

MacNair had been educated in California, at the University of Redlands, newly founded by the Baptists of Southern California. Appositely, as a student he had been a fledgling librarian, tasked with cataloguing the new collection. Like Ayscough, he found the work much to his inclination. He had first come to Shanghai in 1912, and served on faculty at Shanghai's first university, the prestigious St. John's University in Jessfield Park (now the East China University of Political Science and Law), founded by the American Episcopal Mission in 1879. He eventually became Head of the Department of History and Government. As a scholar of Asian history and politics, he was naturally drawn to the Royal Asiatic Society library, and by happy extension, to its librarian; the membership lists of the Society indicate that he became a life member in 1920. He was a frequent guest at the Ayscoughs' home, and spent the years until 1927 mostly in China, then after a year in Seattle became Professor of Far Eastern History and Institutions at the University of Chicago.

MacNair had read *Travels of a Chinese Poet* on the voyage out to Shanghai in the autumn of 1934. The day after he landed, he visited Ayscough for afternoon tea, and finding her wan and in need of a holiday, proposed a tour along the Yangtze, with a pilgrimage to the site of Tu Fu's original Grass Hut in Chengdu. Despite the threat of banditry, the increasing ferocity of Chiang Kai-shek's anti-Communist offensives (the Long March began that year), and reports of attacks on steamers on the Upper Yangtze, Florence, dauntless as ever, agreed—with the concession that she trade the precious opal necklace and earrings she wore each day for glass ones, her 'bandit jewels'.

Together with Ayscough's secretary Gerald Steiner (who was to become MacNair's brother-in-law through marriage to his sister Hazel), they travelled through the gorges by steamer to Chongqing (on Ayscough's first trip in 1922, she had found a little package of opium hidden under her bunk). From Chongqing they flew to Chengdu, and visited the Grass Hut as literary pilgrims. They thought of Tu Fu; maybe they read Ayscough's masterly translation of *Grass Hut Unroofed by Autumn Wind*, maybe MacNair admired the economic evocation of the damp that could rot wood and fabric:

> Presently, of a sudden, wind drops; clouds
>   colour of ink;
> Autumn sky heavy, heavy till yellow dusk,
>   black darkness come.
>
> Wadded quilt many years old, is clammy,
>   and like iron;
> Restive little boy sleeps uneasily; kicks, tears
>   lining.[31]

Undoubtedly there were many, many moments of happiness. It was autumn, but it must have seemed like a second spring:

> Weather clear after rain; we watch small boys
>   bathing in limpid stream.
>
> Fluttering butterflies, a yellow flight, mingle,
>   pursue each other:
> Two lotus blossoms united on one stalk form
>   a natural pair.[32]

Maybe they read Tu Fu's words to a kindred spirit: 'We discuss literature, we smile, we appreciate ourselves.'[33]

That winter MacNair celebrated Chinese New Year with Ayscough at the Grass Hut. Ayscough had made a paper airplane for the kitchen god, so that he might more speedily arrive in the heavens to give his account of the family's behaviour, ensuring the rewards would speedily return to them. The kitchen god of 1935 was an auspicious messenger. Ayscough and MacNair grew closer They took tea together. They addressed each other as 'Mrs. Ayscough' and 'Dr. MacNair'. By his own admission, he could barely tolerate time away from her.

In addition to adjusting to this change of relationship, Ayscough was experiencing what she could of 'New China', especially in regard to the changing status of women. She observed, absorbed, and conducted interviews for her next book *Chinese Women, Yesterday and Today* (1937). She was an acute observer of the fissures and ironies that occurred at the collision of belief systems. Living close to the Jade Buddha Temple, she was able to see the changes wrought to religious devotion. In March 1935 the Buddhist priests, with whom she was friends, invited her to a ceremony for a widow who wished to make an offering for her dead husband:

> There stood a paper house, large enough to walk about in, perfect in every detail. Outside the great gate waited a jinrickshaw for the master's use Inside the house the guest hall was charming, with table, flower vases, pictures; the library had telephone and radio; the bedroom contained curtained bed, chairs, wardrobe, chest of drawers; the kitchen had stove, meat-block, chopper; the bathroom was modern and complete. At the front door stood a White Russian watchman, such as rich Chinese employ all was cunningly fashioned from paper. The widow, a serious, middle-aged woman immersed in her preparations, inspected every detail, sending to the Shadow-World furniture shop for this extra article

and that. A beautiful clock was one addition, a little
hot water bottle which she carefully placed in the bed
being the final perfection. She looked gravely at the
complete erection. Satisfied with the furnishings, she
took handful after handful of paper money, spreading
it generously in every possible nook: on the bed, on
the floors, in drawers, all over the courtyard. In Yin
World her husband's soul should lack nothing that
spirit money could buy.[34]

That spring Ayscough and MacNair took a trip to Japan. Soon
afterwards Florence returned to Guernsey, then travelled to
America, writing to MacNair about her journey in her Jaguar
car, the books they both read, and China. They were married on
Guernsey on 7 September 1935—an outcome that seemed felici-
tously inevitable, but one that surprised American colleagues. A
piqued notice in *The New York Times* remarked that his friends and
associates 'learned of the marriage through a copy of a Guernsey
newspaper'.[35] (*Figure 13*)

The couple settled in Chicago, calling their home at 5533
Woodlawn Avenue, The House of the Wutung Trees, after the
painting by Ren Bonian that Ayscough had catalogued back in
1914 for the Panama–Pacific International Exposition. It was a
robustly American home dating from the 1890s, in the smart
Hyde Park neighbourhood, conveniently opposite the University
of Chicago campus (*Figure 14*). Much of the couple's art collections was housed here, including the 'dogs of Fo' that had guarded
the Grass Hut. With its large garden, gracious reception areas and
spacious library, this house became, in the words of a friend:

a treasure house, museum, and library, a scholar's
workshop, as well as a hearth and home. Their antique
Oriental furniture and rugs, their ceiling-to-floor

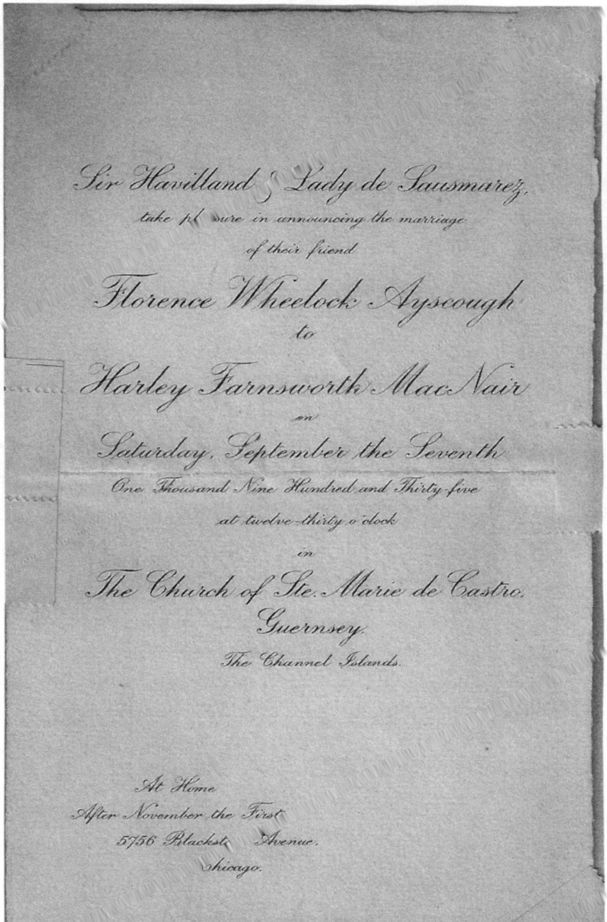

Sir Havilland & Lady de Sausmarez
take pleasure in announcing the marriage
of their friend

Florence Wheelock Ayscough

to

Harley Farnsworth MacNair

on

Saturday, September the Seventh
One Thousand Nine Hundred and Thirty-five
at twelve thirty o'clock

in

The Church of Ste. Marie de Castro,
Guernsey.
The Channel Islands

At Home
After November the First
5756 Blackstone Avenue,
Chicago.

Figure 13 Wedding Announcement for Florence Wheelock Ayscough and
Harley Farnsworth MacNair.

Figure 14 5533 Woodlawn Avenue, Chicago, guarded by the pair of stone 'lion dogs' formerly in the front courtyard of the Grass Hut, Shanghai. Photograph courtesy Laird Books.

> Chinese paintings and scrolls, their moving panels hiding more libraries of Chinese books, the ingeniously lighted cabinet of ancient bronzes and symbolic objects of precious stone … provided, in actuality, a setting for cordiality, considerateness, even coziness, as well as for intellectual, artistic, and spiritual cultivation.[36] (*Figure 15*)

Rather than retreat to library and garden, Ayscough was soon on the lecture circuit once more, speaking to the Society of Women Geographers in January 1936. The following year she published *Chinese Women, Yesterday and Today*. Although at the time, and subsequently, it was criticized for being romanticist and overly concerned with the lives of elite women, it did treat with sympathy and insight the lives of communist and working women, and

Figure 15 Florence Ayscough and Harley MacNair in their Chicago home Christmas card, 1936. Courtesy Laird Books

most significantly, it explained education as the fulcrum for the improvement of the lives of all classes of women.

The life of Qiu Jin the revolutionary martyr was covered at length, not just from secondary sources, but using her daughter (who lived just a mile from the Grass Hut) as an informant. Ayscough also included her own translations of Qiu Jin's poetry. Much earlier, writing to Lowell, she had credited Nung Chu with awakening her to the existence of a body of women's writing; in this publication she was able to introduce an English-speaking audience to much unfamiliar material by women poets, historically remote, yet emotionally immediate:

> Walk alone, sit alone.
> Sing alone, drink a toast alone; then sleep alone.
> Stand by myself, spirit wounded.
> Nothing to be done; slight cold envelops my person.
> My passion, who is aware of it?
> Tears wash away remains of morning make-up, not
>   half is left.[37]

In 1938 Ayscough and MacNair made their last journey to China. It seems by this date the Grass Hut was no longer in Ayscough's possession; the *Desk Hong* directories list the MacNairs at 72 Penang Road in 1936; there is a gap in 1937, and by 1938 the New Shanghai Construction Company occupied this address. From the mid-1930s Penang Road had become increasingly industrialized, and with the addition of lane houses, ever-more densely populated. They added to their antique collections, buying in Beijing what MacNair described as a Qianlong-period wooden screen with a monochrome painting of orchids, and a Tang-dynasty pottery horse.[38] A Beijing dealer also offered them a set of over 100 rubbings from Han-dynasty tomb sculpture in Nanyang. Ayscough published an academic article on these images in *Monumenta*

Serica, a scholarly journal that had recently been founded by a German sinologist and missionary as a forum to enhance Western knowledge of China, and publish the research of Western scholars living in China. In this article she claimed that to her knowledge, nothing had appeared in the English language on these archeological remains that were so important to Chinese scholars.[39]

During this trip Ayscough must have found symptoms that caused enough concern for her to consult a surgeon in Beijing. She was found to have a tumour which was immediately operated on. She recovered well though, and the couple sailed home that summer. On the Indian Ocean at the height of monsoon season, her famously robust constitution allowed her to dress for dinner each evening and composedly progress 'from soup to nuts' while her husband reeled with seasickness.

Back in Chicago both re-immersed themselves in academia. Having worked in China for much of the critical period between 1912 and 1927, MacNair had produced significant scholarship on Chinese nationalism (while Ayscough was being shelled at the French Club in 1927, MacNair and the other faculty at St. John's were preparing against a threatened mob attack on the campus). His *China in Revolution* (1931) was grounded in first-hand experience of the cataclysmic period, just as his new wife's poetry translations were grounded in her experience of place. Now, as Professor of Far Eastern History and Institutions at the University of Chicago, he focused largely on China's international relations, being especially concerned with explaining to an uninformed Western readership the roots of the crisis with Japan.

Ayscough taught a series of public lectures at the University on Chinese history and culture, and continued to publish academic papers. Both Ayscough and MacNair were closely involved with political organizations that supported China during the Japanese occupation. They were also part of the fabric of Chicago's cultural life, and had become donors to the Art Institute of Chicago. On 27 November 1941 Ayscough took part in a museum programme on Han-dynasty art, discussing a collection of rubbings she had donated to the Institute. It was her last public appearance.

The next day she was admitted to hospital, 'for a 2–3 week visit for the heart', but her health further deteriorated, and she remained in hospital throughout the long Chicago winter. In March MacNair wrote to Mary Wilbur, explaining the gravity of her condition:

> When we were in Peking Florence had an operation for a malignant tumor. We hoped that no cells were left. But the trouble has returned and that, with heart troubles, is what is taking her from me … I hope she may go without ever knowing of the return of the Peking trouble. To know that she cannot recover would hurt her so—not that she fears death, but that she enjoys life. … She is the most extraordinarily lovely, stimulating, exquisite and competent person I have ever known. No one else interests me. How can I live without her?[40]

Florence Ayscough died on 24 April 1942. Her memorial service was conducted by the scholarly minister of Chicago's First Unitarian Church, Dr. Von Ogden Vogt. In his address the quality on which he rested was Ayscough's humanism. Throughout her life she had come into contact with belief that was sharply delineated; in Shanghai, Christian missionary activity was one salient aspect of foreign presence in that treaty port. While friendly with many missionaries, she didn't closely identify with missionary circles, preferring a more inclusivist philosophy that eventually identified with Unitarianism. A romantic and idealist, she was also, as Vogt had known her, a pragmatist:

In her life-philosophy she was not simply religious in general but practical and concrete. Though she saw reality and value in many faiths, here in Chicago she became an active member of this Unitarian Church to make her religion specific, and not leave it wandering loose in the clouds. You may be surprised to know that in this connection the thoughts that she most commended were not those of philosophical or artistic or whimsical or poetical character, but those that were the boldest expressions of the need for human justice and for experimentation in things economic.[41]

After her death MacNair often returned to the Unitarian Church on Woodlawn Avenue, just a block from their home. Inside the stone Perpendicular Gothic-inspired building, he took his place where they used to sit, and hoped that the adjoining seat would be empty. Over the next few years, he donated most of their art collections to museums and universities; her collection of 1,292 Chinese-language books was given to the Library of Congress. Recognizing that Ayscough's correspondence with Lowell over production of *Fir-Flower Tablets* gave valuable insights into poetic creativity and the process of translation, he published a volume of their letters, *Florence Ayscough and Amy Lowell: Correspondence of a Friendship* in 1945. The following year he had a collection of essays, letters and tributes privately printed under the title *The Incomparable Lady*. Harley MacNair died on 21 June 1947 from a heart attack triggered by a chronic heart condition.[42]

Afterword
'Here all is alive'[1]

Florence Ayscough wrote long illustrated essays about two places in Shanghai. One was her home at Penang Road; the other was one of her 'favourite haunts'. This wasn't the illustrious Astor House Hotel, or the Country Club in its eleven acres of gracious gardens, or Stehlneek's Gallery, or the Race Club, or anywhere along the Bund with its sweep of showcase architecture. It was the City God Temple in the Old City.

She first lectured on the City God Temple to the Royal Asiatic Society in London in January 1924, and published the text that year in the *Journal of the North China Branch of the Royal Asiatic Society*. An expanded version illustrated by Lucille Douglass is included in *A Chinese Mirror*. The Temple had been of almost no interest to Europeans, and as a place of popular religion dedicated to the spirit of the City Magistrate Qin Yubo—a deity charged with the protection of the city's inhabitants—was largely ignored by Chinese scholars who dismissed it as 'fit for women and the ignorant'. But Ayscough found it the most exuberant place in Shanghai, constantly thronged with people for whom religious expression was a natural part of life. Lacking texts in English, she turned to Nung Chu who, bemused but acquiescent, helped her hunt down Chinese sources to explain the history of the Temple and the nature of this form of popular/Daoist belief. Her essay in *A Chinese Mirror* is part scholarship, part revelry in the sensuous world of incense clouds, gleaming effigies, silver ingots flashing in the furnace, scarlet-clothed children, and processing penitents with weights hooked to their skin.

In 1922, just before Ayscough left Shanghai, a fire raged through the Temple, necessitating a major renovation. While she was in St. Andrews in 1924 another fire threatened the Temple; at the time of writing *A Chinese Mirror* she didn't know whether it still existed. But the Temple had experienced many vicissitudes over its long history, and it survived fire and the Japanese invasion of the city. After the founding of the People's Republic of China, it became a Daoist centre. Shut from the start of the Cultural Revolution, it reopened in 1994.

When the Ho Ho twins invented the abacus, did they imagine it would be used for the accounting of souls? It hangs, enormous, over the entrance to the Temple courtyard, just as Ayscough saw it a century ago. Not that it is a dampener to the spirits of supplicants today. Crowds surge around the brazier, bowing and offering incense. Waves of heat blow arcs of smoke into smarting eyes. Ash rises and settles in smuts on the dresses of immaculately clad children. An attendant tells a woman to stop smoking.

It is a magnanimous place of plenty; Qin Yubo shares his Temple with other deities and the halls of each are piled with the most succulent fruits of the season; peaches, lychees, melons, grapes and tomatoes, as well as offerings that know no season: CDs and White Rabbit candy. In front of the God of Wealth a woman is folding boat-shaped paper ingots with the same deft movements of fingers that Ayscough found so graceful. A boy of maybe eight is nudged to kneel in front of the God of Literature, appealing for a good school performance next year. He resists, for a moment, then abashed and obedient in the way eight-year-olds are, drops to his knees. The adults around him roar with laughter.

Flanking the route to Qin Yubo's inner courtyard are statues of the worthy citizens who had pledged themselves to him as attendants. When Ayscough saw them their robes were dim and their hair beards full of dust and ash. Now they gleam with fresh paint. Beyond them in the courtyard silver yuan coins spin through the air and glisten between the roof tiles. Here are Qin Yubo, his wife, and his parents. They are wooed and adored, and coins thud into the offertory boxes in front of them. Three waggles of clasped hands, and a bow. Waggle, waggle, waggle, bow. Everyone knows these gestures, which in other places would seem an unbroken link with the past, but here must have been faintly remembered, or perhaps reinvented. And then, a rain of coins. Satisfaction.

A young Daoist priest is playing the *dizi* flute. It sounds like birdsong soaring roofwards. When words are unknown or inadequate, incense and music reach the mind of God.

When Ayscough came here, sitting in the shadows with her hand-held camera, she met this absorption, this delight, this confidence that earthly things are pleasing.

It is still possible for a stranger to sit unnoticed in the shade.

Notes

Introduction

1. Ayscough's father, Thomas Reed Wheelock, was Canadian, and hence a British subject. Ayscough's first husband was British. After marrying her second husband, the American scholar Harley MacNair, Ayscough declined to change her citizenship.

2. Peter Sanger, *White Salt Mountain: Words in Time* (Kentville, Nova Scotia: Gaspereau Press, 2005).

3. "Knowledge is pleasure as well as power." William Hazlitt, 'On the Pleasure of Painting, cont.' *Table Talk* (London: John Warren, 1821) 32.

Chapter 1 Shanghailanders

1. This painting may be viewed on the interactive site Virtual Shanghai http://www.virtualshanghai.net/Asset/Preview/dbImage_ID-18669_No-1.jpeg, accessed 30 March 2012.

2. Sanger 28.

3. I am grateful to Eric Politzer for information on John Andrews Wheelock, correspondence with author 31 March 2012.

4. Advertisement, *North China Herald* [cited next as *NCH*] 21 September 1861, p. 150.

5. *NCH* 21 June 1862, p. 99.

6. 'Obituary, T. R. Wheelock', *NCH* 10 January 1920, p. 86.

7. Catherine Mackenzie, 'Florence Wheelock Ayscough's Niger Reef Tea House', *The Journal of Canadian Art History* 23. 1–2 (2002): 55.

8. See Edward Denison and Guang Yu Ren, *Building Shanghai: The Story of China's Gateway* (Chichester: Wiley-Academy, 2006) 66, 251.

9. 'Bubbling Well Road', *Social Shanghai* IV (July–December 1907): 67–72.

10. Florence Ayscough, *Firecracker Land: Pictures of the Chinese World for Younger Readers* (New York: Houghton Mifflin Co., 1932) 5. Subsequent quotes on childhood from this source.

11. Written several decades after Ayscough's childhood, and based on personal recollection, *Firecracker Land* obviously has problems as source material about Shanghai in the 1870s and early 1880s; however, it does present a valuable sensory account (rather than history) of the city in these decades.

12. *NCH* 6 January 1917, p. 27.

13. C. E. Darwent, *Shanghai: A Handbook for Travellers and Residents* (Shanghai: Kelly and Walsh, Ltd., 1920) 168.

14. Florence Ayscough and Amy Lowell, *Fir-Flower Tablets: Poems from the Chinese* [cited next as *FFT*] (Boston: Houghton Mifflin Co., 1921) 2.

15. *FFT* 48.

16. *Firecracker Land* 15–17.

17. Geoffrey Wheelock graduated from Noble and Greenough School, class of 1897. Isa Schaff, School Archivist, correspondence with Lindsay Shen, 28 October 2011. According to his obituary in *The Harvard Crimson*, Thomas Gordon Wheelock also attended this preparatory school. *The Harvard Crimson* 21 April 1902.

18. See Marvin Lazerson, 'Urban Reform and the Schools: Kindergartens in Massachusetts, 1870–1915', *History of Education Quarterly* 11.2 (Summer 1971): 115–42; Sharon Hartman Strom, 'Leadership and Tactics in the American Woman Suffrage Movement: A New Perspective from Massachusetts', *The Journal of American History* 62.2 (September 1975): 296–315.

19. Andrew Sackett, 'Inhaling the Salubrious Air: Health and Development in St. Andrews, N.B. 1880–1910', *Acadiensis* XXV.1 (Autumn 1995): 54–81.

20. Excerpts from *The Beacon* have been compiled by David Sullivan, the Pendlebury Press, and are available online at http://www.seaside. nb.ca/algonquinbook/history/summerpeople/index.html, accessed 22 June 2011.

21. The town's architecture has recently been surveyed in John Leroux and Thaddeus Holownia, *St. Andrews Architecture 1604–1966* (Kentville, Nova Scotia: Gaspereau Press, 2010).

22. *NCH* 10 January 1920, p. 86.

23. 'Ready for College Golf', *The New York Times* 3 May 1901, p. 7.

24. Obituary, Thomas Gordon Wheelock, *The Harvard Crimson*.

25. *Firecracker Land* 23.

26. Isabella Bird, *The Yangtze Valley and Beyond* (New York: G. P. Putnam's Sons, 1899) 46.

27. Eliza Ruhamah Scidmore, *China, the Long-Lived Empire* (New York: Century, 1900) 292.

28. A memorial stained glass window in the church of St. James the Great, Cradley, dedicated by Florence Ayscough, makes clear Francis Ayscough's parentage.

29. Carroll Lunt (ed.). *The China Who's Who 1922* (Shanghai: Kelly and Walsh, Ltd., 1922) 31.

30. Marriage notice, *Boston Daily Globe* 24 December 1898, p. 6.

31. *NCH* 21 November 1898, p. 959; Charles N. Davis, *A History of the Shanghai Paper Hunt 1863–1930* (Shanghai: Kelly and Walsh, Ltd., 1930) 37.

32. 'The Paper Hunt Races', *Social Shanghai* V1 (January–June 1909): 114.

33. *NCH* 14 February 1898, p. 239.

34. *NCH* 21 November 1898, p. 959.

35. *NCH* 17 April 1909, p. 138.

36. Florence Wheelock Ayscough diaries, 1903–7; 1908–11; 1921, Houghton Library, Harvard University, MS Am 2549.

37. *Firecracker Land* 26.

38. Photographs exist in Special Collections, Armacost Library, University of Redlands, CA.

39. *NCH* 18 March 1916, p. 756.

40. See, for example, Hanchao Lu, *Beyond the Neon Lights: Everyday Shanghai in the Early Twentieth Century* (Berkeley: University of California Press, 1999).

41. Ayscough, *The Autobiography of a Chinese Dog* (Boston: Houghton Mifflin Co., 1926) 34.

42. *NCH* 20 June 1908, p. 743.

43. *NCH* 10 July 1909, pp. 86–7.

44. *NCH* 10 February 1917, p. 284.

45. Thomas Gordon Wheelock married the Hollywood actress Mary Astor.

46. Harold M. Otness, '"The One Bright Spot in Shanghai": A History of the Library of the North China Branch of the Royal Asiatic Society', *Journal of the Hong Kong Branch of the Royal Asiatic Society* 28 (1988): 192.

Chapter 2 Images

1. Harley MacNair, *The Incomparable Lady: Tributes and Other Memorabilia Pertaining to Florence Wheelock Ayscough MacNair* (Chicago: privately printed, 1946) 15–16.

2. The Shanghai Literary and Scientific Society was founded in 1857 and within a year the organization was granted affiliation with the Royal Asiatic Society of Great Britain and Ireland.

3. *Firecracker Land* 36.

4. Ayscough, *Friendly Books on Far Cathay: Being a Bibliography for the Student and Synposis of Chinese History* (Shanghai: Commercial Press, 1921).

5. Librarian's Report, *Journal of the North China Branch of the Royal Asiatic Society (JNCBRAS)* 54 (1923): vii.

6. 'The Porcelain Exhibition', *NCH* 14 November 1908, pp. 422–4.

7. Nick Pearce, 'Shanghai 1908: A. W. Bahr and China's First Art Exhibition', *West 86th* 18.1 (Spring–Summer 2011): 22.

8. A. W. Bahr, *Old Chinese Porcelain and Works of Art in China* (London: Cassell and Company, 1911) 8, 10.

9. 'The Porcelain Exhibition', 423.

10. *NCH* 28 January 1922, p. 238.

11. *NCH* 28 May 1921, p. 595.

12. Ayscough, *A Chinese Mirror: Being Reflections of the Reality Behind Appearance* (Boston: Jonathan Cape, 1925) 332.

13. An invitation for submissions was placed in the *NCH* 7 October 1911. The organizing committee included Ayscough and Ferguson as well as several Chinese members.

14. I am grateful to Lara Netting for this information, e-mail to author 9 April 2012.

15. Mary Rankin, 'Nationalistic Contestation and Mobilization Politics: Practice and Rhetoric of Railway Rights Recovery at the End of the Qing', *Modern China* 28.3 (July 2002): 315–61.

16. Hong Zaixin, 'Comprador Liu Songfu and His Collection of Painting in the Modern Market', *The Study of Art History* (艺术史研究) 11 (2009): 483–511.

17. *Firecracker Land* 100. Of course, she may have significantly edited her recollections of Liu Songfu; *Firecracker Land* was, after all, a book for young readers!

18. Quoted in Katharine P. Burnett, 'Inventing a New "Old Tradition": Chinese Painting at the Panama–Pacific International Exposition', *History of Art and History of Ideas* (美术史与观念史) IX (April 2010): 19. I am most grateful to this author for making this article available to me.

19. Office of Shanghai Chronicles (2001), *Chapter 4: Attending International Business Meetings*, http://www.shtong.gov.cn/node2/node2245/node4538/node56987/node57006/node57008/userobject1ai45396.html, accessed 20 October 2011.

20. Burnett 30.

21. For a recent discussion on the formation of Freer's collecting tastes, see Ingrid Larsen, '"Don't Send Ming or Later Pictures": Charles Lang Freer and the First Major Collection of Chinese Painting', *Ars Orientalis* 40 (2011): 6–38.

22. Charles Lang Freer, letter to John Trask, 17 May 1915, Charles L. Freer Papers, Freer Gallery of Art and Arthur M. Sackler Gallery Archives, Smithsonian Institution, Washington, DC.

23. Burnett 46.

24. Charles Baldwin, letter to William Sanders, 6 December 1917. The Cleveland Museum of Art Archives, Records of the Director's Office, Frederic Allen Whiting.

25. I am thankful to Robert Mintz, Mr. and Mrs. Thomas Quincy Scott Curator of Asian Art at the Walters Art Museum, for tracking down the purchase record for the album of modern paintings.

26. Robert Mintz, letter to Lindsay Shen, 26 September 2011.

27. Ayscough, letter to Charles Baldwin, 5 December 1917. The Cleveland Museum of Art Archives, Records of the Director's Office, Frederic Allen Whiting.

28. Ayscough, Preface to *Catalogue of Chinese Paintings Ancient and Modern by Famous Masters* (Shanghai: The Oriental Press, 1914).

29. Ayscough, letter to Charles Baldwin.

30. Harley MacNair (ed.), *Florence Ayscough and Amy Lowell: Correspondence of a Friendship* (Chicago: University of Chicago Press, 1945) 18.

31. See Freer Gallery of Art and Arthur M. Sackler Gallery, 'Song and Yuan Dynasty Painting and Calligraphy', worksheet F1914.53, http://www.asia.si.edu/songyuan/F1914.53/F1914–53.Documentation.pdf, accessed 7 April 2012.

32. *NCH* 16 June 1917, p. 653.

33. Ayscough, letter to Charles Lang Freer, 12 December 1917, Charles L. Freer Papers, Freer Gallery of Art and Arthur M. Sackler Gallery Archives, Smithsonian Institution, Washington, DC.

34. I am most grateful to Ingrid Larsen for information on Lee's family, correspondence with author 10 April 2012.

35. The passages concerning Lee draw on correspondence and a police report now in the Charles L. Freer Papers, series 2.1, box 14, folder 5–6. I am extremely grateful to Rachel Woody for making this available to me.

36. Charles Lang Freer, letter to Florence Ayscough, 13 December 1917, Charles L. Freer Papers, Freer Gallery of Art and Arthur M. Sackler Gallery Archives, Smithsonian Institution, Washington, DC.

37. Ayscough, letter to Frederic Whiting, 27 January 1918. The Cleveland Museum of Art Archives.

38. Ayscough, 'Chinese Painting', *The Mentor* 6.20 (1918): 24.

39. *NCH* 24 February 1917, pp. 404–5.

40. Ayscough, letter to Frederic Whiting, 27 January 1918.

Chapter 3 Words

1. The quote is from Ayscough's description of Li Po, *FFT* lxxx.

2. *FFT* vii.

3. *FFT* v.

4. *Firecracker Land* 108.

5. Amy Lowell, ed., Preface to *Some Imagist Poets: An Anthology* (Boston and New York: Houghton Mifflin Co., 1915) Kindle ebook file location 24.

6. *FFT* 156.

7. Ayscough, 'Written Pictures', *Poetry* 13.5 (February 1919): 268.

8. *FFT* viii.

9. Richard le Gallienne, review of *FFT*, *The New York Times*, 15 January 1922, p. 4.

10. Ayscough, correspondence, *China Journal* 2.6 (November 1924): 528–9.

11. Ayscough, review of *More Translations from the Chinese* by Arthur Waley, *The Chinese Recorder* (May 1920): 354.

12. Ayscough, letter to Mary Matteson Wilbur, 17 November 1930, Mc 561, 24.13 Schlesinger Library, Radcliffe Institute, Harvard University.

13. *FFT* 166.

14. *FFT* 50.

15. Originally published in Pound's *Cathay*, 1915.

16. *Correspondence of a Friendship* 44.

17. *FFT* 123.

18. Witter Bynner and Kiang Kang-Hu, *The Jade Mountain: A Chinese Anthology* (New York: Alfred Knopf, 1931) 199.

19. *Correspondence of a Friendship* 82.

20. *Correspondence of a Friendship* 170.

21. Ayscough, letter to Witter Bynner, 9 April [1921], MS Am 1891 (46) Houghton Library, Harvard University.

Chapter 4 Gardens and the Grass Hut

1. Ayscough described the building of the Grass Hut as 'a liberal education' in *A Chinese Mirror* 19.

2. *Correspondence of a Friendship* 181.

3. *JNCBRAS* 39 (1908): 115; *The Harvard Crimson*, 12 May 1909.

4. *Correspondence of a Friendship* 101.

5. *NCH* 19 June 1920, p. 725.

6. I am grateful to Dorothea Mordan, granddaughter of Albert and Eva Dunlap, for this information.

7. *Incomparable Lady* 8.

8. *NCH* 16 March 1912, p. 712.

9. *NCH* 25 March 1916, p. 789.

10. Dorothee Rihal, 'Foreign-administered Parks in Shanghai: Visual and Spatial Representations of New Forms of Public Open Spaces', http://www.virtualshanghai.net/Article.php?ID=59, accessed 22 October 2011.

11. *NCH* 7 June 1919, p. 655.

12. *NCH* 23 November 1912, p. 502.

13. *NCH* 17 May 1919, p. 460.

14. F. S. A. Bourne, *Gardening in Shanghai for Amateurs* (Shanghai: Kelly and Walsh Ltd., 1915) 23.

15. *Social Shanghai* VIII (July–December 1909): 257.

16. *NCH* 24 April 1915, p. 245.

17. *Social Shanghai* III (January–June 1907): 353.

18. *Social Shanghai* XII (July–December 1911): 246.

19. *NCH* 17 May 1919, p. 461.

20. Emil Bretschneider, 'Botanicon Sinicum', pt. 1 *JNCBRAS* 16 (1881); pt. 2 *JNCBRAS* 25 (1890–1); pt. 3 *JNCBRAS* 29 (1894–5).

21. *NCH* 23 August 1919, p. 493. The writer seems to have mistakenly made reference to Yu Yuen Road (the road running towards Jessfield Park), rather than Yuyuan, the garden.

22. *A Chinese Mirror* 82. The following quotations about the Grass Hut gardens and interiors are from this source.

23. Lin Yutang, 'The Monks of Hangzhou' (1941), Joseph S. M. Lau and Howard Goldblatt (eds.), *The Columbia Anthology of Modern Chinese Literature* (New York: Columbia University Press, 1995): 621–2.

24. *Social Shanghai* 2 (July–December 1906): 59.

25. Arthur de Carle Sowerby, *Nature Notes: A Guide to the Fauna and Flora of a Shanghai Garden* (Shanghai: The China Journal Publishing Co., 1939) 79–80.

26. *Social Shanghai* 12 (July–December 1912): 117–20.

27. An inventory was made of the collection at the time, though it lacks detail and its reliability is questionable. MacNair makes several references to the couple's donations in *Incomparable Lady*.

28. Elinor Pearlstein, 'Color, Life, and Moment', *Art Institute of Chicago Museum Studies* 26.2 (2000): 86.

29. *NCH* 12 April 1913, p. 119.

30. Ayscough, *Waterways of China*, exhibition catalogue of pastels by Lucille Douglass, 30 March–11 April 1925, n.p.

31. *NCH* 12 February 1921, p. 605.

32. *NCH* 29 April 1922, p. 570.

33. MacKenzie 45.

34. *Incomparable Lady* 57.
35. *Incomparable Lady* 57.
36. 'Amy Lowell and Sevenels', MS Am 2088 Houghton Library, Harvard University.
37. *Correspondence of a Friendship* 199.
38. *Autobiography of a Chinese Dog* 42.
39. *Acadia Bulletin* 14.2 (November 1928–January 1928): 8. Available online http://openarchive.acadiau.ca/cdm4/document.php?CISOROOT=/AAB&CISOPTR=4455&REC=4, accessed 20 June 2011.

Chapter 5 After China

1. *Correspondence of a Friendship* 200.
2. Ayscough, *Travels of a Chinese Poet: Tu Fu, Guest of Rivers and Lakes*, vol. 2 (London: Jonathan Cape, 1934) 212. Ayscough grouped her English words to correspond with the Chinese characters, without retaining their order.
3. See Mackenzie for details of this project.
4. *Correspondence of a Friendship* 224.
5. *Correspondence of a Friendship* 225.
6. These are among the Honorary Members listed in the *JNCBRAS* 52 (1921): 237.
7. *The Society of Woman Geographers: A Register of Its Records in the Library of Congress*, available at http://lcweb2.loc.gov/service/mss/eadxmlmss/eadpdfmss/2005/ms005005.pdf, accessed 14 May 2009.
8. *The Geographical Journal* 71.1 (January 1928): 111.
9. Sanger 60.
10. Ayscough, letter to Mary Matteson Wilbur, 16 Nov. [1926], Mc561, 24.13 Schlesinger Library, Radcliffe Institute, Harvard University.
11. *Incomparable Lady* 19.
12. Ayscough, *Tu Fu: The Autobiography of a Chinese Poet* (London: Jonathan Cape, 1929) 232.
13. Ayscough, letter to John Livingston Lowes, 31 July 1927, MS Am 1493 Houghton Library, Harvard University.

14. Ayscough, letter to Wilbur, 5 January 1928, Schlesinger Library.

15. Ayscough, letter to Wilbur, 27 March 1928, Schlesinger Library.

16. *Tu Fu: The Autobiography* 159.

17. *Tu Fu: The Autobiography* 175. Lynn Pan has pointed out that Ayscough has mistranslated the word for 'countless' as 'few'.

18. *Journal of the Royal Asiatic Society of Great Britain and Ireland* 1 (1930): 213.

19. Transcript in A. M. Sullivan Papers, Special Collections Research Center, Syracuse University Library.

20. *Incomparable Lady* 50.

21. Ayscough, letter to Wilbur, 17 November 1930, Schlesinger Library.

22. *Correspondence of a Friendship* 226.

23. Ayscough, letter to Wilbur, Christmas 1931, Schlesinger Library.

24. Ayscough, letter to Wilbur, 5 May [1931], Schlesinger Library.

25. *Incomparable Lady* 8.

26. *Incomparable Lady* 31.

27. I would like to thank Sue Laker of the Priaulx Library, St. Peter Port, Guernsey, for this information.

28. Ayscough, letter to Wilbur, 29 December [undated], Schlesinger Library.

29. Ayscough, letter to Lowes, 10 July 1943, Houghton Library.

30. He says this explicitly in *Incomparable Lady* 5.

31. *Travels of a Chinese Poet* 104.

32. *Travels of a Chinese Poet* 101.

33. *Tu Fu: The Autobiography* 305.

34. Ayscough, *Chinese Women, Yesterday and Today* (Boston: Houghton Mifflin Co., 1937) 74.

35. 'Wedding in Britain for Mrs. Ayscough', *The New York Times* 26 September 1935, p. 20.

36. Maurice T. Price, 'Harley Farnsworth MacNair (22 July 1891–22 June 1947)', *The Far Eastern Quarterly* 8.1 (November 1948): 54.

37. *Chinese Women* 197.

38. *Incomparable Lady* 39.

39. Ayscough, 'An Uncommon Aspect of Han Sculpture Figures from Nan-yang', *Monumenta Serica* 4 (1934–40): 335.

40. Harley MacNair, letter to Wilbur, 15 March 1942, Schlesinger Library.

41. *Incomparable Lady* 82.

42. Although Price gives a date of 22 June, Harley's sister Hazel Steiner makes it clear that he died on 21 June. Hazel Steiner, letter to Mary Wilbur, 21 August 1947, Schlesinger Library.

Afterword

1. *A Chinese Mirror* 397.

Selected Bibliography

Ayscough, Florence, and Amy Lowell. *Fir-Flower Tablets*. Boston: Houghton Mifflin Co., 1921.

Ayscough, Florence. *A Chinese Mirror: Being Reflections of the Reality Behind Appearance*. Boston: Jonathan Cape, 1925.

———. *The Autobiography of a Chinese Dog*. Boston: Houghton Mifflin Co., 1926.

———. *Tu Fu: The Autobiography of a Chinese Poet*. London: Jonathan Cape, 1929.

———. *Firecracker Land: Pictures of the Chinese World for Younger Readers*. New York: Houghton Mifflin Co., 1932.

———. *Travels of a Chinese Poet: Tu Fu, Guest of Rivers and Lakes*, vol. 2. London: Jonathan Cape, 1934.

———. *Chinese Women, Yesterday and Today*. Boston: Houghton, Mifflin Co., 1937.

Baker, Barbara (ed.). *Shanghai: Electric and Lurid City*. Hong Kong: Oxford University Press, 1998.

Bickers, Robert. *Britain in China: Community, Culture and Colonialism, 1900–49*. Manchester: Manchester University Press, 1999.

———. *The Scramble for China: Foreign Devils in the Qing Empire 1832–1914*. London: Allen Lane-Penguin Books Ltd., 2011.

Bickers, Robert and Christian Henriot (eds.). *New Frontiers: Imperialism's New Communities in East Asia, 1842–1953*. Manchester: Manchester University Press, 2000.

Selected Bibliography

Bland, J. O. P. *Houseboat Days in China*. Hong Kong: Earnshaw Books, 2008 (first pub. 1909).

Cahill, James. *The Lyric Journey: Poetic Painting in China and Japan*. Cambridge, MA: Harvard University Press, 2002.

Clarke, David. *Chinese Art and Its Encounter with the World*. Hong Kong: Hong Kong University Press, 2011.

Clifford, Nicholas. *Spoilt Children of Empire: Westerners in Shanghai and the Chinese Revolution of the 1920s*. Hanover, NH: University Press of New England, 1991.

Denison, Edward, and Guang Yu Ren. *Building Shanghai: The Story of China's Gateway*. Chichester: Wiley-Academy, 2006.

Djordjevic, Nenad. *Old Shanghai Clubs and Associations*. Hong Kong: Earnshaw Books, 2009.

French, Paul. *Through the Looking Glass: China's Foreign Journalists from Opium Wars to Mao*. Hong Kong: Hong Kong University Press, 2009.

Hibbard, Peter. *The Bund Shanghai: China Faces West*. Hong Kong: Odyssey Books and Guides, 2007.

Hinton, David. *Mountain Home: The Wilderness Poetry of Ancient China*. New York: New Directions, 2005.

Hobart, Alice Tisdale. *Within the Walls of Nanking*. London: Jonathan Cape, 1928.

Huang, Yunte. *Transpacific Displacement: Ethnography, Translation, and Intertextual Travel in Twentieth-Century American Literature*. Berkeley: University of California Press, 2002.

Keswick, Maggie. *The Chinese Garden: History, Art and Architecture*. Cambridge MA: Harvard University Press, 2003.

Lau, Grace. *Picturing the Chinese: Early Western Photographs and Postcards of China*. Hong Kong: Joint Publishing (H.K.) Co., 2008.

Lu, Hanchao. *Beyond the Neon Lights: Everyday Shanghai in the Early Twentieth Century*. Berkeley: University of California Press, 1999.

Mackenzie, Catherine. 'Florence Wheelock Ayscough's Niger Reef Tea House', *The Journal of Canadian Art History* 23. 1–2 (2002).

MacNair, Harley (ed.). *Florence Ayscough and Amy Lowell: Correspondence of a Friendship*. Chicago: University of Chicago Press, 1945.

———. *The Incomparable Lady: Tributes and Other Memorabilia Pertaining to Florence Wheelock Ayscough MacNair*. Chicago: privately printed, 1946.

Maugham, W. Somerset. *On a Chinese Screen*. Hong Kong: Oxford University Press, 1986 (first pub. 1922).

Pan, Lynn. *Shanghai Style: Art and Design Between the Wars*. Hong Kong: Joint Publishing (H.K.) Co., 2008.

Pott, F. L. Hawks. *A Short History of Shanghai*. Shanghai: Kelly and Walsh, Ltd., 1928.

Sanger, Peter. *White Salt Mountain: Words in Time*. Kentville, Nova Scotia: Gaspereau Press, 2005.

Sowerby, Arthur de Carle. *Nature Notes: A Guide to the Fauna and Flora of a Shanghai Garden*. Shanghai: The China Journal Publishing Co., 1939.

Spence, Jonathan. *The Search for Modern China*. New York: W.W. Norton and Co., 1990.

———. *The Chan's Great Continent: China in Western Minds*. London: Penguin Books, 2000.

Valder, Peter. *Gardens in China*. Portland: Timber Press, Inc., 2005.

———. *The Garden Plants of China*. Portland: Timber Press, Inc., 2005.

Wasserstrom, Jeffrey. *Global Shanghai, 1850–2010: A History in Fragments*. New York: Routledge, 2009.

Wood, Frances. *No Dogs and Not Many Chinese: Treaty Port Life in China 1843–1943*. London: John Murray, 1998.

———. *The Lure of China: Writers from Marco Polo to J. G. Ballard*. Hong Kong: Joint Publishing (H.K.) Co., 2009.

Yoshihara, Mari. *Embracing the East: White Women and American Orientalism*. New York: Oxford University Press, 2003.

Yue, Meng. *Shanghai and the Edges of Empire*. Minneapolis: University of Minnesota Press, 2006.

Index

Index